THE
Provençal
TABLE

THE
Provençal
TABLE

JANE NEWDICK AND MAXINE CLARK

PHOTOGRAPHY BY SANDRA LANE

EBURY PRESS
LONDON

First published in 1997

1 3 5 7 9 10 8 6 4 2

Text © Jane Newdick 1997
Recipes © Maxine Clark 1997
Photographs © Sandra Lane 1997

First published in the United Kingdom in 1997 by Ebury Press
Random House, 20 Vauxhall Bridge Road, London SW1V 2SA

Random House Australia (Pty) Limited
20 Alfred Street, Milsons Point, Sydney,
New South Wales 2061, Australia

Random House New Zealand Limited
18 Poland Road, Glenfield, Auckland 10, New Zealand

Random House South Africa (Pty) Limited
Endulini, 5a Jubilee Road, Parktown 2193, South Africa

Random House UK Limited Reg. No. 954009

A CIP catalogue record for this book is available from the British Library.

ISBN 0 09 182003 0

Designed by Alison Shackleton
Photography by Sandra Lane
Styling by Jane Newdick
Food styling by Maxine Clark

Printed and bound in Singapore by Tien Wah Press

CONTENTS

THE TABLE

France is still a country where one can eat well almost anywhere and where meals are an important part of every day, whether eaten at home or in a restaurant. Most people's best memories of French food are linked to lazy days on holiday, when there is time to enjoy relaxed meals with family or friends. In Provence these occasions will probably have taken place outdoors, perhaps on a terrace or under the welcome shade of a vine covered arbour. The food will have been memorable, the wine abundant and the style of the table and the pieces used on it will have completely fitted the mood. The Provençal table is sometimes elegant, often colourful and always functional. No time is spent on fussy details or complicated arrangements, just simple plates, cloths, cutlery and flowers alongside wonderful food. There are dozens of ideas in this section to help you achieve the Provençal look so that the concentrated feeling of sun and colour, generosity of spirit and warmth can translate to your home no matter how far away your table is from Provence.

CHINA

The china used on the Provençal table is a very distinctive part of it. Several types are recognized far from this region of France as being characteristic of the area. To create your own table settings, though, you do not necessarily have to restrict yourself to china made in Provence; rather, you can use things that are in the spirit of the region and look right with the food. It is hard to tell which comes first – the style of china or the food that is eaten from it. Both elements are connected, and are more or less the key to achieving the right feel to a table setting.

The food of Provence is often colourful but never complicated. Intense flavours are combined with more mellow ones, both of which spring from the surrounding land and sea. A Mediterranean cuisine, it differs greatly from that of many other regions of France where better soil and higher rainfall produce richer ingredients. The agriculture of Provence is sparse and the soil not very fertile, and this is combined with low rainfall but plenty of light and sun. Winters, apart from in the coastal area, can be quite cold and there is little permanent pasture. Staple foods include olive oil, herbs of all kinds, tomatoes, saffron, fish, lamb and beef, abundant vegetables and fruit, game, good bread, but little dairy produce. There are wonderful regional luxuries, such as honey made by the bees that forage in the flower-scented garrigue and lavender fields, and almonds from the hillier areas to the north, which are used in many puddings, cakes and sweet confections. Cheese is likely to be made from goat's or sheep's milk while butter is imported from northern areas of France, as there are no dairy cows in Provence. The food is robust, fresh, colourful and earthy, beautiful to look at and extremely healthy and delicious to eat. The nearer you go to the Italian border the more influences there are from Italian cooking.

Meals are generally served in a relaxed and informal way, though some traditional feasts demand more formality. In summer, most meals are eaten at a table outside under a shady tree or a vine-covered arbour, and are likely to have been lovingly prepared at home from good, fresh produce. The choice of food is very much governed by the seasons and what is best in the market that day or ready to be picked in the garden. Wine is drunk at every meal from a choice of young local wines, which are almost always served chilled even if they are light red.

For a Provençal-style table setting, the china needs to be robust and simple in character to complement the food served on it. Often quite strong colours are used for glazes, two of the most famous being a glowing golden yellow and a clear leaf or emerald green. Provence has an abundant supply of red clay which is suitable for making pottery, so many towns have developed their own specialized products. The most common style of pottery in the region is a fairly thick earthenware, or faïence, which is both distinctive and practical. Besides the well-known yellow and green opaque-glaze versions there are also ranges with a white glaze and multi-coloured designs and others with marbled patterns. Much of the faïence of the early eighteenth century was made in a restrained pattern of blue on white but since then more colour has appeared, though there is still a tradition for beautiful plain white or cream pottery. Plain plates inevitably show off food better than highly patterned ones. A simple cream plate with an interesting wavy edge makes a perfect background for any food, so if buying bright yellow plates seems too daring or you are worried they might limit your options for different table settings, go for a simpler choice.

All shades of blue look fresh and pretty, whether used for the entire glaze or as a fine pattern, such as a row of lines or checks around the rim of a bowl.

CLOCKWISE FROM TOP LEFT: CLEAR BLUE GLAZE INSPIRED BY THE SKY AND THE SEA WORKS BEST ON SIMPLE SHAPES • BREAKFAST BOWLS ON A BLUE CHECK CLOTH AWAIT FOAMING HOT CHOCOLATE OR COFFEE • A CLASSIC FRENCH SHAPE TO A GITANE BLUE JUG • A MARINE FEEL TO SMART NAVY BLUE AND WHITE NAPKINS AND SHINY BLUE ESPRESSO CUPS

Blue and white always has a contemporary feel and people never seem to tire of it. It is particularly suitable for big breakfast bowls, cups for serving chocolate or coffee, and salad bowls and serving dishes. Green salad looks good in a blue bowl and so do brightly coloured vegetable salads such as ones containing tomatoes or peppers. Darker blue and white designs look crisp and fresh.

The Provençal repertoire contains quite a few soups, as well as dishes with plenty of liquid or sauce which need to be served in deep bowls. Wide shallow soup plates show off the food well but let it cool quickly. Smaller, deeper soup bowls are excellent for cream soups or ones that don't contain large chunks of food, and the liquid remains very hot for a long time. Both shapes of bowl can double up for serving puddings, while soup plates are the best dishes for eating pasta from. Large dinner plates are obviously needed for every meal and perhaps a smaller size, too, for salad or cheese or for serving desserts. Most food looks better served on a larger plate than is really necessary rather than being squashed into too small a space.

Many Provençal dishes are served at table straight from the container in which they were cooked. Think of vegetable tians or rich stews and daubes. These do not need to be decanted into different dishes and, if they were, would lose most of their charm, as well as the delicious crisp brown bits round the edges. Simple glazed terracotta pots are ovenproof and sometimes even suitable for use over a flame, and are practical for all kinds of cooked foods. It is useful to have a few serving dishes for grilled or roasted foods or ones that need to be arranged prettily before they are dished out. Tiny dishes and bowls are ideal for serving hors d'oeuvres and accompaniments, such as mayonnaise, olives, capers, cornichons or anchovies. They are even useful for putting coarse salt in for the table.

CLOCKWISE FROM TOP LEFT: ROUND AND COMFORTING GLAZED CASSEROLES ARE THE PERFECT SHAPE FOR *DAUBES* AND STEWS • GREEN AND BLUE ARE OFTEN COMBINED AND HERE THERE IS AN ADDED SPLASH OF RED DECORATION • BRIOCHE DOUGH RISES SLOWLY IN AN ANCIENT TERRACOTTA MOULD • TERRACOTTA BOWLS GLAZED IN YELLOWS AND GREENS ARE STURDY AND PRACTICAL

GLASS

A warm climate generally means that plenty of liquid is drunk, and Provence is no exception. Even after a leisurely game of boules in the village square, everyone will gather to drink something refreshing and reviving – partly as an excuse to stay a little longer and talk some more. The French would not dream of eating a main meal, whether lunch or dinner, unaccompanied by wine of some kind. Provençal wines are light and refreshing, designed to be drunk young, chilled and in quantity. They are easy to drink at any time, so there is great temptation to imbibe quite a few glasses in the course of a day. There are no really great wines produced in the area, though of course these are brought in from other regions of France. The most popular local wines are light reds and a deep rosé, which suit the style of Provençal food to perfection as they can hold their own against intense, gutsy flavours. The simplest and most appropriate glasses for this type of wine are sturdy, cheap and cheerful tumblers, the sort of everyday glasses that can be bought from any shop or supermarket and are resilient enough to be carried outside from the kitchen and then back time and time again. This kind of glass looks equally at home on a rough wooden table or a brightly patterned cloth. Stemmed wine glasses are fine for special occasions and more elegant indoor meals but they are a little impractical for relaxed family meals round the kitchen table or outdoors on the terrace. If a stemmed glass is used it is likely to be a very simple, classic shape of the kind you would find in any good restaurant. Tumblers have the great advantage, too, of being able to be stacked for carrying, or you can invest in a wire carrying basket which holds half a dozen glasses, enabling them to be taken anywhere with ease.

Tumblers can be updated by choosing ones in coloured rather than plain glass. This makes the table more visually exciting and is unlikely to upset any

A COLLECTION OF OLD FRENCH PRESERVE POTS, EACH ONE VERY SLIGHTLY DIFFERENT FROM THE NEXT

wine traditionalists if you stick to serving vins de pays from them. Of course no-one says you must drink wine, and tumblers are just as suitable for quaffing plain water, citron pressé or any soft drink you choose. Use these simple, colourful glasses for flowers on the table, too, or choose small versions for night-time dining, when they can be lit with a nightlight or a small candle dropped into each. These little table lights are the easiest and most effective way of lighting the table and you will have no problems with the breeze blowing out candles. As the light source glows, the coloured glass lights up in a magical way. Leave them out on the table for evening meals and replace the nightlights inside regularly as they burn down.

Generally, glass for the Provençal table tends to be functional rather than decorative but this doesn't mean that things don't look good too. Provençal cooks are thrifty and make the most of seasonal produce when it is plentiful. They like to preserve fruits and vegetables in all sorts of ways and, more often than not, the results are kept in glass storage jars. Originally everything would have been stored in earthenware jars such as the famous green or yellow olive jars of the region or plain cream or brown smaller storage jars. Making an air-tight seal on these was not easy, so the invention of a foolproof device was welcomed. The advent of cheap, mass-produced glass containers for storing food meant far better hygiene and greater convenience for the cook. The biggest advantage of all was that you could see how things looked through the gleaming glass. The classic French wide-necked glass storage jar with a rubber seal and spring-clip lid has been popular for years, as it is very practical and efficient and can be re-used time and time again. Glass jars filled with preserved tomatoes and whole vegetables are a common sight in Provençal storecupboards, alongside honey, jam, herb pastes, tapenades and all kinds of delicious concoctions designed to lengthen the life of foods. A jar with straight sides and a wide neck is easier to fill and empty, especially if the foods being preserved are quite large. Because the jars are so handsome, people tend to take them

SPARKLING GLASS PRESERVING JARS GLEAM WITH GOOD THINGS

straight to the table when needed rather than dishing the contents out into yet another container. These simple preserving jars can be used for straightforward storage of dry goods, too, and are attractive enough to display on any kitchen shelf, so they do not have to be hidden away in a cupboard.

Jams and preserves look very pretty, with their glowing, jewel-like colours. The classic French glass jam jar has a wide neck slightly tapering to the base. As fewer people preserve fruit at home nowadays, old versions of these jars can often be found at fleamarkets and broquantes, and some of the nicest ones are elegant enough to use as dishes on the table.

Other types of glass for the Provençal table might include a salad bowl for the all-important green salad. Glass is a pretty and up-to-date choice for this and far more attractive than an oily old wooden bowl. A glass salad bowl will double up for other purposes too and can also be used for fruit salads. Choose a large bowl so there is plenty of room to toss the salad leaves with the vinaigrette. Too small a bowl makes this very difficult to do well and results in a badly dressed salad. The French way is usually to pour the dressing into the bowl first, then toss in the leaves, turning them over in the dressing with a long-handled spoon and fork. Each leaf should end up lightly coated in the dressing rather than drenched in it.

Provençal glass, then, is first and foremost functional and always practical but there are some pieces that are more valuable and decorative. The lovely bubbly Biot glass is typical of the south of France, though it is quite expensive these days. It comes in several different pale shades, of which the prettiest are sea greens and translucent turquoise. Biot glass is definitely for special occasions rather than daily trips out to the terrace, though it is so beautiful that one might be tempted to use it as often as possible.

CLOCKWISE FROM TOP LEFT: BLUE AND GREEN COMBINED ON THIS MODERN TUMBLER IS VERY PROVENÇAL • SLIGHTLY FROSTY GLASS HAS AN ICY QUALITY, WHICH SUITS THE FRILLY SALAD LEAVES WELL • USE AN INJECTION OF STRONG COLOUR TO BRING A PLAIN TABLE TO LIFE • COLLECT TOGETHER LOTS OF DIFFERENT GLASS JARS IN ONE COLOUR FOR LITTLE CANDLES AND NIGHTLIGHTS

LINEN AND CUTLERY

For many people the fabrics of Provence are the brightly coloured, busily patterned cotton prints that are still made in the south of France by companies such as Souleiado. They have been produced here for hundreds of years and were originally influenced by imports of fabric from India to the port of Marseilles. In the seventeenth century these Indian fabrics were remarkable for their colourfastness and they rapidly became popular all over France, until they were banned because the businesses of indigenous fabric manufacturers were suffering. Permission was given for them to be imported from India once more a century later, by which time French manufacturers had perfected their own methods of producing colourful printed cottons in the Indian style, using small wooden hand blocks. These days they are printed in far larger quantities using modern methods.

As these fabrics have been exported all over the world, most of us are very familiar with them. Exuberant and fun, they suit relaxed table settings, especially outdoor ones, but they also have the knack of bringing a saturated sunlight feel to tables indoors even on the gloomiest winter day. Use them with caution, though, as their dominant colour and pattern is likely to take over, making everything else on the table fade into the background. If you want to achieve the look without using too much fabric, choose Provençal-print napkins or placemats only and keep everything else plain and simple. You could have a plain blue, green or yellow tablecloth and add splashes of colour with complementary patterned napkins. The different ranges of these fabrics are designed to co-ordinate and to be mixed and layered. As well as quite complicated floral or paisley motifs and large-scale patterns there are also simple little prints, usually made with a single repeated design on a small scale and in fewer colours. Provençal boutis – finely quilted bed covers made using typical

BLUE AND WHITE JUST HAS TO BE THE FRESHEST EVER COMBINATION, HERE WITH YELLOW
FOR ADDED ZING

Provençal prints – make wonderful solid tablecloths for special occasions.

Colour is important to the Provençal look. You only have to think of street markets awash with the brilliance of fruit and vegetables, or views of the sapphire-coloured sea through flowering yellow mimosa. Even the paint colours or the vivid glazed tiles on kitchen walls and floors vary from deep, chalky blues to pinks and terracotta. However, colour is always used with care in Provence, and there are certain classic combinations. A deep, strong blue, very clean and clear and sometimes with a hint of mauve to it like a hyacinth, is often combined with yellow. Red is another popular colour, often used in combination with pure white or more subtly with cream. Yellow is everywhere, the sunniest, most golden yellow like the yolk of a free-range egg. This may be combined with a strong leaf green or an earthier rust or burgundy. These colours never seem to date and always look fresh and new. They are colours for strong light and bright sunshine but can look equally good in a northern kitchen.

Provençal fabrics are invariably made from natural fibres which wash well time and time again. However fast a dye is, though, it may fade dramatically if left out in strong sunshine day after day, so remember not to leave a cloth on the table outside after the meal is finished. Remember, too, that white cloths used on tables outdoors in full sunshine can produce a glare that is really off-putting for the people gathered round to eat.

Linen is a wonderful natural fabric for table coverings. From the finest damask to coarse, handwoven stuff, it makes a beautiful background to any table setting. Antique linen can still be found in France because so much was made by hand a century or so ago. It is remarkably tough and looks good after every wash, but has recently become popular again and rather expensive.

All over France it is possible to find simple check fabrics. Usually they consist of small blocks of a colour plus white, and different versions are available in red, yellow, blue and green. There is a beautiful soft fabric which is double woven to produce these very neat, squared checks and it is wonderfully dense,

SHADES AND PATTERNS OF GREEN CAN COMBINE IF YOU USE ENOUGH OF THEM TOGETHER yet folds and hangs very gently. Sometimes the check design has a more complicated patterned border or panel alongside it. Blue and white checks, stripes, block prints, weaves or jacquards all have the right Provençal feel, especially with golden yellow for a real contrast.

Provençal cutlery is sturdy and well made. To create the right look for the Provençal table, use traditionally designed old silver plate on a grand scale or go for bright new pieces or cutlery with smart wooden handles. Anything too delicate or detailed will look wrong with the solid china and chunkier pieces that make up the rest of the table. You do not need a battery of equipment – just a knife, fork and spoon for most everyday meals. Soup is only ever served for dinner, never lunch, and special soup spoons are not often used. Many meals finish with fruit rather than dessert, so you may just need knives for bread, cheese and main courses and forks for main courses and salads. Provençal meals are all about delicious simple food and wine, not ceremony and formality. When a special meal does have many different courses, cutlery for each one might be provided in a grand house or in a restaurant, but in normal homes you might be expected to keep the cutlery you are given at the start of the meal.

There are many ranges of plastic-handled cutlery and a huge variety of colours to choose from, including deep burgundy red and cool white or cream. Wooden-handled cutlery needs more care and generally should be handwashed. The French must have always liked colourful cutlery: examples can still be found of old bone-handled cutlery dyed in quite strong colours. Mix and match colourful cutlery according to your taste. Contrast handles with the cloth and china on the table or keep everything in the same shades. If you are uncertain what looks good with what, one solution is to choose plain blackriveted-handled pieces of cutlery. These strong, rustic pieces suit the Provençal table perfectly.

CLOCKWISE FROM TOP LEFT: A MODERN VISION OF CLASSIC BEECHWOOD-HANDLED CUTLERY • IMMACULATE, STIFFLY STARCHED NAPKINS FOR SPECIAL OCCASIONS ONLY • CRISP RED ON WHITE FOR KITCHEN AND TABLECLOTHS IS VERY SMART AND VERY FRENCH • BONE AND ROSEWOOD-HANDLED CUTLERY DRAINS IN AN OLD CHEESE STRAINER

FLOWERS AND DECORATIONS

The people of Provence love flowers. Even the smallest outdoor market has a stall or two devoted to them, filled with large and colourful blooms from all over the world as well as many supplied by local growers. Provence is always associated with certain flowers, partly because of the time a century or so ago when large crops of scented blooms were grown commercially as raw material for the fragrance industries, which were mostly clustered around the town of Grasse. Roses, jasmine, lavender and violets were all cultivated on a grand scale but, sadly, these days the cost of growing and harvesting is prohibitive and many of the pure essential flower oils are imported from other countries.

On warm spring days in Provençe the sweet, heady scent of mimosa fills the air. Mimosa trees are often planted in towns, particularly ones along the coast, as well as in more rural parts of the province. Later in the year, lines of lavender wind along the edges of fields and across terraced land. This shrub is still grown in quantity, not least to provide excellent forage for honey bees. Fields of sunflowers are now a common sight all over France but at one time they were more concentrated in the south. Grown as an oil crop originally and now part of a huge agro-industry, an offshoot of this is that they can be found regularly as a cut flower in shops and stalls, and are the perfect way to bring an instant touch of Provence to the table.

Wild flowers are everywhere in Provence – some bright, like scarlet, papery field poppies, and many just small, scrubby herbs which make up the richly scented maquis. We sometimes forget that herbs are beautiful to look at as well as to eat, and a small posy composed of a variety of different leaves makes a beautiful table decoration. Choose herbs with prettily shaped leaves or with a certain amount of colour variation, such as a mix of greyish green, brighter green and purple. Along the same theme there is no reason not to use

PREVIOUS PAGE: A BIG JUG OF FLOWERS MANAGES TO LOOK ELEGANT YET RELAXED OUTDOORS • OPPOSITE: FRENCH LAVENDER SMELLS LIKE NO OTHER AND LOOKS GOOD JUST AS IT IS IN A LITTLE SHEAF

the most decorative fruits and vegetables as table decorations instead of or as well as flowers. Tiny fennel bulbs complete with their feathery green tops, or rosy red and white radishes with fat green leaves, may be served as part of a crudité course to be eaten with garlic-laden aïoli but they also look good displayed in little bunches or laid on a pretty plate in a complementary colour as a centrepiece. Artichokes, when fresh and young, with a few leaves still attached, are exquisite to look at with their mix of purple and green and silvery-grey leaves, every bit as lovely as an exotic flower. Pile a little collection of them on a stand or plate and save them so that you can cook them later.

Few people can resist the appeal of lavender, whether growing fresh in the garden and fields or dried and tied into little scented bunches for winter decorations. An ancient plant, it is found growing wild in Provence, though cultivated versions are used commercially. It makes a lovely cut flower when fresh and is particularly good mixed in with other summer flowers such as roses and sweet peas, particularly if these have little or no scent of their own. The more heavily scented lavenders are usually a mid-mauve when in bloom, while the darkest, purple-flowered varieties sadly lack the true powerful lavender fragrance.

Another flower commonly seen in Provence, though only ever in gardens, is the plain and simple pelargonium, or zonal geranium. Often grown in pots, this vivid, cheerful flower shines out from every courtyard, balcony and row of steps but somehow one never tires of the bright scarlets and pinks glowing in the dazzling sunshine. Another plant that grows well in a tub or pot and which is distinctively French is the single white marguerite. Pots of these starry white daisies make wonderful instant table decorations and, if you plan to eat outdoors regularly, Provençal-style, then you could leave a pot of marguerites on the table outside as a centrepiece. Paint the pot in a colour to suit your table setting or stand it in a colourful cachepot or a plain basket.

CLOCKWISE FROM TOP LEFT: SHAGGY MARIGOLDS IN A CLEAR GREEN VASE ADD POOLS OF SUNLIGHT TO A SHADY TABLE • SUBTLE SHADES OF PURPLE, SILVER AND GREEN FROM FRESH YOUNG ARTICHOKES AND LOTS OF DIFFERENT HERBS • MIMOSA IS WELCOME IN LATE WINTER AND EARLY SPRING • BRIGHT, SHINING DAISIES ARE WHITER THAN WHITE

BASKETS, WOOD, METAL AND DETAILS

Apart from basic china, linen and cutlery, all kinds of other items are needed to complete the well-dressed Provençal table. Of course these details are dictated by the kind of meal you are going to serve and where and why it is being held. Everyday meals, and especially relaxed ones held outdoors, demand simplicity in the food to be served and the bits and pieces required to serve it. Although there is no great formality at most Provençal meals there is an enormous amount of tradition. This runs through every aspect of life in Provence and is possibly more pronounced in this region than in any other part of France.

Breakfast is usually brief and simple but lunch is an important meal. Since it is held during the hottest part of the day, this is where the table set up under an arbour of vines or in the deep shade of a large leafy tree becomes invaluable. To save a lot of running backwards and forwards between kitchen and garden, the table is set simply. A cloth may be thrown over it and minimal cutlery laid out. A glass carrier is often used to bring tumblers out to the table. These little wire baskets have spaces for six or so glasses and are often made in the decorative twisted wirework that is very typical of this area. Larger ones are available, too, for carrying bottles outdoors. Old wire carriers are beautiful, with their wobbly lines and charming extra squiggles and details, but there are new versions to choose from, too, including light but stiff woven basket versions. As well as being practical, these look very pretty standing on the table. Wine and other drinks are usually served straight from their bottles but sometimes a large jug or carafe takes their place.

Traditionally the forested mountains of northern Provence have provided the raw material for wooden items, whether larger-scale buildings and structures or small, everyday items such as boards and bowls. The abundant olive groves have also played their part in producing a distinctive wood, which is

THE PRETTIEST WIRE GLASS CARRIER APPEARS TO FLOAT ON A YELLOW CHECK CLOTH

deeply grained and marked with swirling darker veins on a rich golden background. The root of the olive is used for smaller pieces which demand a hard, close-grained wood. Wooden boards are invaluable for chopping and preparing food and for transporting food from kitchen to table. Good, heavy, solid ones are best for working on and they must be heavy enough not to slip while you are using them. Boards for bread or cheese or for carrying a hot dish to table should be thinner and lighter than a chopping board and may have a handle or be paddle shaped to make carrying them easier. A selection of these boards in different sizes is useful to have, especially for outdoor meals, because they are sturdy and practical and will not easily be spoiled or broken. Wood is also turned on a lathe to make bowls of all sizes, which are useful to have in the kitchen for holding coarse sea salt or other dry goods, or olives and similar foods which are usually only eaten in small quantities. There is something homely and comfortable about wooden dishes that have aged and mellowed down the years, slowly improving with time and becoming friends of the family. Buy them when you see them, as they have just the right kind of rusticity for the Provençal table. Large wooden salad bowls, however, are more of an acquired taste; most people these days prefer a large china or glass bowl which can be kept clean easily and makes the salad look fresh and appetizing.

Another very typical southern French material is basketware. This may be made of fine willow or reed or wider slats of roughly cut sweet chestnut. Chestnut wood is made into small baskets, and sometimes chairs and other larger pieces, too, and fits very well into a Provençal garden. Baskets are still used every day by many people in Provence. Where people walk and work locally there are always things to be carried. We are used to throwing everything loose into a car and forget that in many places people may still shop daily at the market on foot or go to gather fresh vegetables from a kitchen garden a little way from the house. There is still a great tradition for local people to go out with baskets to collect the wild herbs that grow everywhere in the area. No

OLD SWEETMEAT DISPLAY BASKETS HOLD ALMOND CALISSONS AND REAL FRUIT JELLIES one has yet come up with a better container than a basket for so many jobs. Baskets are great for the table, too – for example, lined with a napkin they make the best container for bread while, covered with a layer of fresh vine leaves, they are the perfect place to put cheeses. Small baskets with lids are sensible for outdoor meals as they can be closed to protect or keep fresh whatever is inside. A large, strong, flattish basket is useful for carrying linen, cutlery and china out to the table for meals outdoors, and fruit and vegetables always look good piled into a natural basket, where they are kept airy and in good condition until you need them. Baskets made from wire, apart from the bottle carriers mentioned earlier, are very common in France. These may be designed for a specific purpose such as shaking a salad dry or, shaped like a dome, they are used to protect food from insects.

We are all familiar with wire mesh cooling trays but the French make prettier small versions to use as trivets or small stands. Old pieces tend to be of a more complicated and finer design than new ones and are still to be found in flea markets, brocantes and antique shops. The wire, which is usually black, makes strong graphic shapes and is very decorative when set against colourful backgrounds or combined with earthier materials. Solid metal pieces are typically Provençal, too. Think of sturdy pewter, with its ancient gleaming surface. It was once used for many purposes, including cutlery, but has fallen out of fashion over the years, though old pieces are still owned and cherished. Fresh fruits and bright colours glow against this subtle background and it is quite practical to use everyday for serving food in. Look out for dessert stands or deep bowls which will hold piles of fruit such as dark-bloomed grapes or chalky purple figs. All these traditional materials have a feel and texture that is ideally suited to the Provençal table. Their timeless appeal means that they look good mixed with the newest pieces and never seem out of place.

CLOCKWISE FROM TOP LEFT: DUSKY GRAPES AND FIGS DISPLAYED ON BURNISHED PEWTER • PROVENÇAL BASKETS ARE PRACTICAL AND PRETTY • BLACK WIREWORK SALAD SHAKER AND COOLING TRAYS • A SIMPLE ROUND WOODEN BOARD WITH A STYLISH HANDLE IS PERFECT FOR A RUSTIC LOAF

THE RECIPES

Provençal food is instantly suggestive of sun-ripened flavours and fresh, healthy ingredients. The recipes in this section include traditional Provençal dishes such as Bouillabaisse and Daube de Boeuf, and many others with an authentic but up-to-date regional appeal, such as Seared Tuna Niçoise or a Couscous Salad. The Provençal market place provides the inspiration for many of the dishes – newly-caught fish, brightly-coloured vegetables, Niçoise olives, fresh herbs and even lavender flowers are used, along with such staples as olive oil and anchovies. Having set the scene, you can now create the full flavour of the Provençal table.

SOUPS

BOUILLABAISSE

This famous soup was originally *'un plat de pauvre'* – a poor man's dish. There is a great deal of argument about what makes an authentic bouillabaisse. This version uses a wide selection of fish for a full flavour, simmered with saffron, leeks, fresh tomato and sun-dried tomato for a rich smoky taste, then strained to give a wonderful orange broth. Spicy, garlicky rouille is whisked in just before serving.

Serves 6–8

1.8 KG/4 LB MIXED FISH (SEE BELOW), CLEANED BUT LEFT WHOLE

1 MEDIUM COOKED CRAB

450 G/1 LB FRESH MUSSELS

150 ML/¼ PINT/⅔ CUP PROVENÇAL OLIVE OIL

4 MEDIUM LEEKS, TRIMMED AND SLICED

2 MEDIUM FENNEL BULBS, TRIMMED AND SLICED

700 G/1½ LB RIPE RED PLUM TOMATOES, ROUGHLY CHOPPED

4 GARLIC CLOVES, UNPEELED BUT LIGHTLY CRUSHED

0.4 G ENVELOPE OF SAFFRON THREADS

30 ML/2 TBSP SUN-DRIED TOMATO PASTE (SEE PAGE 101) OR 6 SUN-DRIED TOMATOES IN OIL, DRAINED AND ROUGHLY CHOPPED

5 ML/1 TSP FENNEL SEEDS

SMALL PIECE OF DRIED ORANGE PEEL (SEE PAGE 100)

2.3 LITRES/4 PINTS/5 QUARTS FISH STOCK

SALT AND FRESHLY GROUND BLACK PEPPER

15 ML/1 TBSP PASTIS OR OTHER ANISEED APERITIF (OPTIONAL)

1 QUANTITY ROUILLE (SEE PAGE 89)

GRILLED COUNTRY BREAD, TO SERVE

Using a heavy knife, chop the fish into large chunks, bones and all. Place in a large bowl. Pull the legs off the crab, crack them with a cleaver and add to the fish. Pull the main shell from the abdomen. Pull off the spongy gills or 'dead men's fingers' and remove the little plastic-like stomach sac. Chop the shell and abdomen into large chunks and add to the fish. Scrub and de-beard the mussels, discarding any damaged ones or any that do not close tightly when tapped. Place the mussels in a bowl of cold water.

In a large pot, heat the olive oil and add the leeks and fennel. Cook gently for about 5 minutes, until beginning to soften, then add the tomatoes, garlic, saffron, tomato paste or sun-dried tomatoes, fennel seeds and dried orange peel. Pour in the fish stock, cover, and boil for 20 minutes to emulsify the olive oil. Add the fish and crab, bring to the boil again, half cover and simmer for a further 20 minutes. Drain the mussels and add to the soup. Cover and simmer for 5 minutes, then strain the entire soup into another pan through a fine sieve or a colander lined with muslin. Discard the solids as they will have given up all their flavour by now. Taste and season the soup, reheating to serve. Just before serving, stir in the Pastis, if using, and whisk in 60 ml/4 tbsp of rouille. Serve with plain grilled or barbecued country bread, and the remaining rouille in a pot for those who like more garlic and spice!

FISH CHOICE

Choose at least four varieties – the more variety, the more intense the flavour. However, oily fish such as salmon, herring or sardines are not suitable.

EUROPEAN FISH SELECTION:

Conger eel, cod, common crab, green shore crab (favouille), red gurnard (rouget grondin), haddock, hake, halibut, John Dory, monkfish, mussels, ocean perch, plaice, red mullet, shark, skate, slipper lobster (cigales de mer) or raw prawns, sole, swordfish, rascasse, weever, whiting, wrasse.

AMERICAN FISH OPTIONS:

Black bass, striped bass, croaker, cunner, drum, grouper, haddock, hake, halibut, ocean catfish, ocean perch, sea perch, porgy, redfish, red snapper, rock cod, rockfish, scrod, sculpin, sea robin, sea trout, sheepshead, shrimp, skate wings, soft shell crab, spot, stargazers, tautog, tom cod.

ICED TOMATO SOUP AU PISTOU

A fresh tomato soup rather like a Spanish gazpacho, served with a purée of basil, oil and garlic stirred in at the last moment.

Serves 6

900 G/2 LB FRESH RIPE RED TOMATOES
2 SWEET RED PEPPERS, CORED, SEEDED AND
ROUGHLY CHOPPED
2 GARLIC CLOVES, PEELED AND CHOPPED
5 ML/1 TSP HARISSA (SEE PAGE 105) OR 1 SMALL
RED CHILLI, SEEDED AND FINELY CHOPPED
90 ML/6 TBSP PROVENÇAL OLIVE OIL

30 ML/2 TBSP SHERRY VINEGAR
600 ML/1 PINT/2½ CUPS TOMATO JUICE
125 G/4 OZ/⅔ CUP PITTED BLACK OLIVES, CHOPPED
SALT AND FRESHLY GROUND BLACK PEPPER
A HANDFUL OF TORN MINT LEAVES
600 ML/1 PINT/2½ CUPS CRUSHED ICE, TO SERVE
SPRIGS OF FRESH MINT, TO SERVE

PISTOU

4 GARLIC CLOVES, PEELED
SALT
50 G/2 OZ/1 PACKED CUP FRESH BASIL

150 ML/¼ PINT/⅔ CUP EXTRA VIRGIN PROVENÇAL
OLIVE OIL

Remove the core from the tomatoes with a small sharp knife. Plunge the tomatoes into boiling water for 5–10 seconds, then remove and refresh in cold water. Slip off the skins. Cut in half around the middle and gently squeeze out the seeds. Place the flesh in a food processor with the sweet red peppers, garlic and Harissa or chilli. Blend to a rough purée, then transfer to a bowl and stir in the olive oil, vinegar, tomato juice and olives. Season to taste, then cover and chill in the refrigerator for at least 3 hours or overnight.

Meanwhile, make the pistou. Pound the garlic with a good pinch of salt in a pestle and mortar until creamy. Add the basil and pound until paste-like, then stir in the olive oil a little at a time until well amalgamated. Add salt and pepper to taste if necessary. Alternatively, you can place the garlic, basil and a pinch of salt in a food processor and blend until smooth, then, with the machine still running, add the olive oil in a steady stream until well blended. (To store the pistou, transfer it to a jar and pour a layer of olive oil on top to exclude the air. It will keep like this for a week in the refrigerator.)

When you are ready to serve the soup, stir in the mint leaves and crushed ice, taste and adjust the seasoning. Serve in chilled glass bowls with a spoonful of pistou and a sprig of mint in each, accompanied simply by some good bread.

AÏGO BOULIDO

This garlic broth is often served as a pick-me-up and is meant to be very restorative and a great hangover cure! I find the traditional way of making the soup with water and a couple of cloves of garlic rather insipid, so I make mine with concentrated chicken or duck stock (or canned consommé), masses of garlic and a veritable bouquet of herbs.

Serves 6

2 HEADS OF GARLIC, PEELED AND LIGHTLY CRUSHED
225 G/8 OZ LEEKS, TRIMMED AND SLICED
225 G/8 OZ MILD ONIONS, PEELED AND FINELY SLICED
A VERY LARGE BOUQUET OF FRESH BAY, THYME, SAGE AND ROSEMARY, OR 3 DRIED BOUQUETS GARNIS

1.7 LITRES/3 PINTS/7½ CUPS STRONG CHICKEN OR DUCK STOCK OR CONSOMMÉ
3 EGG YOLKS
15 ML/1 TBSP SHERRY VINEGAR
SALT AND FRESHLY GROUND BLACK PEPPER
45 ML/3 TBSP CHOPPED FRESH CHIVES

Place the garlic, leeks and onions in a large saucepan, add the herbs and stock and bring slowly to the boil. Simmer uncovered for about 40 minutes, skimming from time to time.

Strain the soup through a fine sieve into another saucepan. Discard the onions, leeks and herbs. Pick the garlic out of the sieve and mash to a paste with the egg yolks and vinegar. Stir a little of the hot soup into this paste, then whisk it into the rest of the soup. Reheat until almost at boiling point; the soup should thicken very slightly. Taste and season, then stir in the chopped chives. Serve the soup as it is or with a poached egg slipped into it, sprinkled with grated cheese. Sliced cooked waxy potatoes are also good heated in this soup.

NOTE

For an even richer soup, sauté the garlic, onions and leeks in olive oil or duck or goose fat. This can be bought in jars and cans in France but is also worth rendering yourself at home. Cut off the skin and excess fat from a raw duck or goose and cut into small pieces. Place in a saucepan with 60 ml/4 tbsp cold water and bring to the boil. Turn down the heat and simmer very slowly for 1½–2 hours, then strain through a fine sieve into a clean jar. Cool, then cover and refrigerate. It keeps well in the fridge and makes roast potatoes taste ambrosial!

SOUPE VERTE AU PISTOU

A beautiful soup in shades of green, lifted with the sunny flavours of garlic, basil and golden olive oil, which are pounded to a paste, or pistou, very much like Italian pesto. The variations are endless, so use whatever vegetables are in season. This soup is best reheated and eaten the next day once the flavours have had time to meld, although it will not be so colourful.

Serves 6

125 G/4 OZ/⅔ CUP DRIED FLAGEOLET BEANS

45 ML/3 TBSP PROVENÇAL OLIVE OIL

1 MEDIUM ONION, PEELED AND SLICED

3 MEDIUM LEEKS, TRIMMED AND THINLY SLICED

1 FENNEL BULB, TRIMMED AND SLICED

1 LARGE POTATO, PEELED AND FINELY DICED

A FEW SPRIGS OF FRESH THYME

2 BAY LEAVES

225 G/8 OZ FRESH SPINACH, WASHED AND SHREDDED

350 G/12 OZ BROCCOLI, DIVIDED INTO FLORETS

2 MEDIUM COURGETTES (ZUCCHINI), DICED

125 G/4 OZ/1 CUP GREEN BEANS, CUT INTO SHORT LENGTHS

125 G/4 OZ/⅔ CUP SHELLED YOUNG BROAD BEANS (FAVA BEANS), INNER SKINS REMOVED (USE PEAS IF BEANS ARE NOT AVAILABLE)

75 G/3 OZ/½ CUP DRIED VERMICELLI, BROKEN INTO SHORT LENGTHS

FRESHLY GRATED PARMESAN OR GRUYÈRE CHEESE, TO SERVE

PISTOU

50 G/2 OZ/1 PACKED CUP FRESH BASIL

4 GARLIC CLOVES, PEELED

2 RIPE TOMATOES, SKINNED AND SEEDED

50 G/2 OZ/½ CUP PARMESAN CHEESE, FRESHLY GRATED

150 ML/¼ PINT/⅔ CUP PROVENÇAL OLIVE OIL

SALT AND FRESHLY GROUND BLACK PEPPER

Soak the flageolet beans in cold water overnight. The next day, drain and transfer to a saucepan. Cover with cold water and bring to the boil, then cover and simmer for about 45 minutes – 1 hour, until almost tender. Drain.

Heat the oil in a large pan and add the onion, leeks and fennel. Cook gently for 10 minutes, until beginning to soften, then add the cooked beans, potato, herbs and enough water to cover – about 1.4 litres/pints/2½ pints/6cups. Bring to the boil, cover and simmer for 30 minutes, until the flageolet beans begin to disintegrate.

Meanwhile, make the pistou. Pound the basil, garlic and tomatoes with a pestle and mortar until paste-like, then add the Parmesan. Stir in the olive oil a little at a time until well amalgamated. Add salt and pepper to taste. Alternatively, place the basil, garlic, tomatoes and Parmesan in a food processor and blend until smooth. With the machine still running, pour in the olive oil in a steady stream. Transfer to a bowl to serve.

Add the spinach, broccoli, courgettes (zucchini), green beans, broad beans (fava beans) or peas, and broken vermicelli to the soup and cook for another 10–15 minutes. All the vegetables and the pasta should be very tender. Taste and check the seasoning. Serve piping hot with a dollop of pistou in each serving and a sprinkling of grated cheese.

ROAST PUMPKIN SOUP

A creamy soup made with one of the great vegetables of the area. The Provençal pumpkin is round, ridged and brown-skinned and has bright orange flesh inside. Serve the soup in a hollowed-out pumpkin for fun!

Serves 6–8

700 G/1½ LB PUMPKIN
6 GARLIC CLOVES, UNPEELED
150 ML/¼ PINT/⅔ CUP PROVENÇAL OLIVE OIL
2 MEDIUM LEEKS, TRIMMED AND SLICED
1 CELERY STICK, TRIMMED AND SLICED

1 MEDIUM POTATO, PEELED AND DICED
1.4 LITRES/2½ PINTS/6 CUPS VEGETABLE STOCK OR
 WATER
SALT AND FRESHLY GROUND BLACK PEPPER
60 ML/4 TBSP CHOPPED FRESH PARSLEY

Scrape out the seeds from the pumpkin and cut off the skin. Cut the flesh into large cubes. Place in a roasting pan with the garlic cloves and toss with half the olive oil. Do not crowd the pan – use 2 if necessary. Roast in an oven preheated to 200°C/400°F/Gas Mark 6 for about 30 minutes, until very tender and beginning to brown.

Heat the remaining olive oil in a large saucepan and add the leeks, celery and potato. Cook over a gentle heat for 10 minutes, until just beginning to brown and soften. Pour in the stock or water and bring to the boil, then cover and simmer until the potato is tender.

When the pumpkin and garlic are ready, cool slightly, then pop the garlic cloves out of their skins. Add the pumpkin and garlic to the leek, celery and potato mixture, bring to the boil and simmer for 10 minutes. Purée in a blender or pass through a mouli-légumes and return to the pan. Taste and season with salt and plenty of freshly ground black pepper. Add extra stock or water if the soup seems too thick. Reheat to serve and stir in the parsley.

BREAD AND PASTRY

PAN BAGNAT

This is perfect picnic food – all the ingredients are layered into a flat loaf, wrapped and weighted down overnight. Carry the loaf to the picnic and cut it into quarters to reveal its juicy multi-layers of Provençal goodies! Pan Bagnat literally means 'bathed bread' – bread moistened with olive oil and other ingredients. If really keen, use the Fougasse recipe on page 50 to make your own loaf of bread or rolls, cutting a criss-cross pattern on top before baking.

Serves 2–4

1 FLAT ROUND COUNTRY LOAF (A LARGE BAGUETTE WOULD WORK JUST AS WELL)

75 ML/5 TBSP PROVENÇAL OLIVE OIL

1 GARLIC CLOVE, PEELED AND CRUSHED

45 ML/3 TBSP SHERRY VINEGAR OR WINE VINEGAR

SALT AND FRESHLY GROUND BLACK PEPPER

3 LARGE RIPE TOMATOES, THINLY SLICED

45 ML/3 TBSP PISTOU (SEE PAGE 43) OR A HANDFUL OF FRESH BASIL LEAVES

6 RADISHES, FINELY SLICED

1 MEDIUM SWEET ONION, PEELED AND FINELY SLICED

12 ANCHOVY FILLETS IN OIL, DRAINED

30 ML/2 TBSP TAPENADE (SEE PAGE 85) OR 12 PITTED BLACK OLIVES

1 LARGE SWEET RED PEPPER, ROASTED, PEELED, SEEDED AND SLICED

Slice the loaf horizontally in half and pull out any doughy centre. Heat the olive oil and garlic together in a small pan until just warm, then whisk in the vinegar, salt and pepper. Sprinkle this over the cut sides of the loaf. Arrange the tomato slices on one half of the bread and drizzle with the pistou or scatter with basil. Cover with the radishes, onion and anchovies, dot with tapenade or olives and cover with slices of roasted pepper. Carefully place the other half of bread on top and press down lightly. Wrap tightly in greaseproof paper (wax paper) and aluminium foil or a clean cloth. Place a board or tray on the loaf, weighting it down with a can or jar, and leave for at least 2 hours or overnight. Slice to serve.

FOUGASSE

This is the pretty, leaf-shaped bread found all over Provence. It can be flavoured with aniseed, herbs, olives, anchovies, walnuts or crisp fried lardons of bacon. An egg-enriched version is eaten at Christmas.

Makes 1 large loaf

450 G/1 LB/4 CUPS STRONG WHITE FLOUR (BREAD FLOUR)

25 G/1 OZ FRESH YEAST (COMPRESSED YEAST)

5 ML/1 TSP SALT

10 ML/2 TSP PROVENÇAL OLIVE OIL, PLUS EXTRA FOR BRUSHING

Sift 100 g/3½ oz/scant 1 cup of the flour into a medium bowl. Cream the yeast in a small bowl with 150 ml/¼ pint/⅔ cup water at blood temperature. Make a well in the flour and pour in the yeast mixture. Whisk well, then cover and leave in a warm place for 1 hour until risen and foamy.

Sift the remaining flour and the salt into a large bowl. Make a well in the centre, pour in the yeast mixture and mix together. The dough should be medium soft – if it is too dry, add a little extra warm water. Turn out on to a floured surface and knead for 10 minutes, until smooth. Place in an oiled bowl, cover with a damp cloth and leave to rise in a warm place for about 1 hour or until doubled in size.

Knock back the risen dough, turn out on to a clean work surface and knead in the olive oil. Knead in any flavourings at this stage, too. Flour the work surface and roll the dough out to an oval about 5 mm/¼ inch thick. Carefully transfer to a floured heavy baking sheet (cookie sheet). Cut 6 slits with a sharp knife to resemble the veins of a leaf. Open up the slits a little and cover with a damp tea towel. Leave to rise in a warm place for about 1 hour, until puffy.

Heat the oven to 230°C/450°F/Gas Mark 8 and place a roasting tin (roasting pan) of hot water on the bottom of the oven. Carefully brush the loaf with olive oil and bake in the middle of the oven for 25–30 minutes, until crisp and brown. Cool on a wire rack.

PISSALADIÈRE

This Provençal onion 'pizza', baked in a rectangle with an olive and anchovy lattice, is found in every boulangerie and pâtisserie in the Midi. It can be served warm or cold.

Serves 6

45 ML/3 TBSP PROVENÇAL OLIVE OIL, PLUS EXTRA
    FOR DRIZZLING
1.4 KG/3 LB MILD ONIONS, PEELED AND VERY THINLY
    SLICED
3 GARLIC CLOVES, PEELED AND SLICED
400 G/14 OZ CAN OF CHOPPED TOMATOES

5 ML/1 TSP HARISSA (SEE PAGE 105)
5 ML/1 TSP DRIED HERBES DE PROVENCE
SALT AND FRESHLY GROUND BLACK PEPPER
90 ML/6 TBSP BLACK OLIVE PASTE
ABOUT 10 ANCHOVY FILLETS, HALVED LENGTHWAYS
12–18 SMALL BLACK OLIVES (NIÇOISE, IF POSSIBLE)

YEAST PASTRY

7.5 G/¼ OZ FRESH YEAST (COMPRESSED YEAST),
    10 ML/2 TSP DRIED ACTIVE YEAST, OR ½ SACHET
    EASYBLEND (INSTANT) YEAST
PINCH OF SUGAR
PINCH OF SALT

150 G/5 OZ/1¼ CUPS PLAIN WHITE FLOUR (ALL-
    PURPOSE FLOUR)
50 G/2 OZ/¼ CUP BUTTER
1 EGG, BEATEN

Heat the oil in a large saucepan and add the onions and garlic. Stir well to coat with the oil, then stir in the tomatoes and harissa. Cover tightly and simmer over a very low heat until the onions are meltingly soft – about 1–1½ hours – stirring from time to time to prevent them sticking. Do not allow them to colour. Stir in the dried herbs and transfer the mixture to a sieve placed over a bowl to drain off the excess liquid. This will be used to make the base. To make the yeast pastry, cream fresh yeast (compressed yeast) in a bowl with the sugar, then whisk in 30 ml/2 tbsp of the warmed reserved tomato and onion liquid. Leave for 10 minutes until frothy. For dried yeasts, use according to the manufacturer's instructions.

Sift the flour into a bowl with the salt and rub in the butter. Make a well in the centre, then pour in the beaten egg and the yeast mixture. (If using Easyblend (instant) yeast, add to the flour before rubbing in the butter and then stir in 30 ml/½ tbsp of the reserved onion liquid with the egg.) Mix together with a round-bladed knife and then with your hands until it comes together in a soft dough. Knead for a couple of minutes in the bowl until smooth, then place the bowl and dough inside a large polythene bag and leave to rise for 1 hour or until doubled in size.

Knock down the dough, knead lightly, then roll out to line a shallow rectangular 20 x 28 cm/8 x 13 inch tin (jelly roll pan), bringing the dough well up the sides. Spread the olive paste over the base, then the onion mixture, then arrange the anchovies in a lattice over the surface. Drizzle with a little oil and bake in an oven preheated to 190°C/375F°/Gas Mark 5 for about 1 hour, until the pastry is golden and crisp. Arrange the olives over the top and serve.

ONION AND ANCHOVY TARTS

These deliciously creamy tarts are scented with rosemary, both in the pastry and the filling.

Serves 6

8 GARLIC CLOVES, PEELED

450 ML/¾ PINT/2 CUPS CRÈME FRAÎCHE OR DOUBLE
   CREAM (HEAVY CREAM)

2 SPRIGS OF FRESH ROSEMARY, PLUS EXTRA TO GARNISH

3 MEDIUM RED ONIONS, PEELED AND FINELY SLICED

15 ML/1 TBSP SHERRY VINEGAR OR WINE VINEGAR

45 ML/3 TBSP PROVENÇAL OLIVE OIL

6 ANCHOVY FILLETS, DRAINED AND FINELY CHOPPED

3 EGGS, BEATEN

SALT AND FRESHLY GROUND BLACK PEPPER

**PÂTE
BRISÉE**

100 G/3½ OZ/7 TBSP BUTTER, SOFTENED

15 ML/1 TBSP CHOPPED FRESH ROSEMARY

1 EGG YOLK

200 G/7 OZ/1¾ CUPS PLAIN WHITE FLOUR (ALL-
   PURPOSE FLOUR)

5 ML/1 TSP SALT

To make the pastry, place the butter, rosemary and egg yolk in a food processor and blend until smooth. Sift the flour and salt on to a sheet of greaseproof paper (wax paper). Shoot the flour into the food processor while it is running and blend until JUST combined. If the pastry is a little dry, add about a tablespoon of iced water to moisten. Tip out on to a floured work surface and knead gently until smooth. Form into a ball, flatten and wrap in cling film (plastic wrap). Chill for at least 30 minutes.

Allow the pastry to come to room temperature before rolling it out and using to line 6 individual 10-cm/4-inch loose-bottomed tartlet tins (tart pans). Prick the bases with a fork and bake blind for 15 minutes in an oven preheated to 190°C/375°F/Gas Mark 5, until set and beginning to brown. Leave to cool.

Place the whole garlic cloves in a small pan with the cream. Bruise the rosemary sprigs with the flat of a large knife and add to the cream. Bring to the boil, cover and simmer very gently for 20 minutes, until the garlic is soft.

Meanwhile toss the sliced onions with the vinegar. Heat the olive oil in a pan, add the onions and cook gently for 10 minutes or until softened. Stir in the anchovies.

Lift the rosemary out of the hot cream mixture and mash the garlic into the cream with a fork or potato masher. Cool slightly, then beat in the eggs. Season well. Spread the onion mixture over the base of each tart, then pour over the cream. Top each with a sprig of rosemary and bake in an oven preheated to 190°C/375°F/Gas Mark 5 for 20–25 minutes, until set and lightly browned. Serve warm or at room temperature.

FISH

BRANDADE DE MORUE

This is a delicious salt cod and potato purée flavoured with parsley and walnut oil. It makes a great starter, very traditional at Easter and on Christmas Eve. It is made with salt cod, not dried salt cod which is too strong for some and needs soaking forever! Choose a fairly plump piece of salt cod that has been cut from the middle of the fish. If salt cod is not available, brandade can be made very successfully with smoked cod or haddock, which does not need soaking.

Serves 8

450 G/1 LB SALT COD, SOAKED FOR AT LEAST 24 HOURS IN SEVERAL CHANGES OF WATER

450 ML/¾ PINT/2 CUPS MILK AND WATER MIXED

SPRIG OF FRESH THYME

1 BAY LEAF

8 PEPPERCORNS

450 G/1 LB FLOURY POTATOES, PEELED AND CUT INTO CHUNKS

150 ML/¼ PINT/⅔ CUP BEST PROVENÇAL OLIVE OIL

3 GARLIC CLOVES, PEELED AND CRUSHED

45 ML/3 TBSP CHOPPED FRESH PARSLEY

FRESHLY GROUND BLACK PEPPER

WALNUT OIL, FOR DRIZZLING

GRILLED, TOASTED OR FRIED BREAD, TO SERVE

Place the cod skin-side up in a pan with the milk and water, thyme, bay leaf and peppercorns. Bring to the boil, then remove from the heat and leave to cool in the liquid. Meanwhile, boil the potatoes for about 20 minutes until tender, then mash well. Keep warm.

Strain the liquid from the cod and reserve. Flake the cod, discarding the skin and bones. Heat the oil in a saucepan until a piece of stale bread will sizzle in it. Add a spoonful of cod and stir well. Keep adding the cod, spoonful by spoonful over a medium heat, beating well until it is all used up. Stir in the garlic and parsley, then beat in the mashed potatoes. Add enough of the reserved cooking liquid to give a soft, creamy consistency. Season heavily with freshly ground black pepper, then pile into a dish and drizzle with walnut oil before serving on grilled, toasted or fried bread.

NOTE

I once served individual dollops of this with jellied Bloody Marys set in very tall dariole moulds – it was a wild success!

SQUID WITH RAITO

Some say raito was brought to Marseilles by Phoenician traders. Traditionally served with white fish, it is a rich red wine and tomato sauce with garlic, herbs, capers and olives. The secret of this sauce is to reduce it very well over a long period of time.

Serves 4

45 ML/3 TBSP PROVENÇAL OLIVE OIL

1 LARGE SWEET ONION, PEELED AND CHOPPED

2–3 GARLIC CLOVES, PEELED AND CHOPPED

30 ML/2 TBSP PLAIN WHITE FLOUR (ALL-PURPOSE FLOUR)

450 ML/¾ PINT/2 CUPS DECENT RED WINE

450 G/1 LB RIPE TOMATOES, ROUGHLY CHOPPED, OR 400 G/14 OZ CAN CHOPPED TOMATOES

30 ML/2 TBSP TOMATO PURÉE

50 G/2 OZ/½ CUP WALNUTS OR ALMONDS, FINELY GROUND (OPTIONAL)

1 BAY LEAF

5 ML/1 TSP DRIED THYME

2.5 ML/½ TSP EACH DRIED ROSEMARY AND FENNEL SEEDS

PINCH OF GROUND CLOVES

SALT AND FRESHLY GROUND BLACK PEPPER

30 ML/2 TBSP CAPERS IN VINEGAR, DRAINED AND RINSED

16 SMALL BLACK OLIVES (NIÇOISE, IF POSSIBLE)

60 ML/4 TBSP CHOPPED FRESH PARSLEY

700 G/1½ LB SMALL SQUID

Heat the oil in a flameproof casserole, add the onion and garlic and cook gently for 15–20 minutes, until very soft but not coloured. Stir in the flour, then the red wine, an equal quantity of boiling water, the tomatoes, tomato purée, nuts, if using, and the herbs and spices. Bring to the boil and simmer uncovered for at least 1 hour, until reduced to about 750 ml/1¼ pints/3 cups. Taste and season with salt and pepper, then purée in a blender or pass through a sieve. Stir in the capers, half the olives and half the parsley.

Meanwhile, clean the squid, leaving the tubes whole but cutting off the heads from the tentacles. Heat a ridged cast-iron griddle pan and fry the squid for 2 minutes on each side. The griddle must be searing hot. Transfer the cooked squid to a plate.

To serve, either add the squid to the sauce, reheat gently and serve in shallow bowls garnished with the remaining olives and parsley, or spoon a little sauce on to individual plates and pile the squid on top in a mound. Scatter the reserved olives and parsley on top.

BOURRIDE

This version of the famous Provençal fish stew, which originated in Sète, is more refined than some. Traditionally the fish steaks and fillets are kept whole and served alongside the thickened soup, moistened with a little of the broth. The recipe here looks more attractive and has more of a chowder feel to it – rich and creamy.

Serves 6
1.4 KG/3 LB THICK FILLETS OR STEAKS OF FIRM WHITE FISH

1 QUANTITY AÏOLI (SEE PAGE 84)

3 EGG YOLKS

45 ML/3 TBSP DOUBLE CREAM (HEAVY CREAM)

1 BAGUETTE, SLICED AND GRILLED OR FRIED IN OLIVE OIL, TO SERVE

BROTH
1 LITRE/1¾ PINTS/4 CUPS FISH STOCK (DON'T USE WATER; THE SOUP WILL TASTE TOO THIN)

150 ML/¼ PINT/⅔ CUP DRY WHITE WINE

2 LEEKS, TRIMMED AND SLICED

2 LARGE CARROTS, PEELED AND SLICED

2 SLICES OF LEMON

A STRIP OF DRIED OR FRESH ORANGE PEEL (SEE PAGE 100)

1 BAY LEAF

5 ML/1 TSP FENNEL SEEDS

LARGE SPRIG OF FRESH THYME

SALT AND FRESHLY GROUND BLACK PEPPER

Place all the ingredients for the broth in a large pan and bring to the boil. Turn down the heat and simmer uncovered for 20 minutes. Strain into another pan and discard the vegetables and flavourings. Taste the broth and season well. Carefully place the fish in the broth and heat slowly until the liquid is barely simmering. Cook the fish for 10 minutes or until just done. Lift out the fish and flake the flesh, discarding the skin and any bones.

Spoon half the aïoli into a serving dish and set aside. Beat the remaining aïoli with the egg yolks and cream and whisk into the broth a little at a time. Reheat without boiling (or it will curdle), stirring all the time, until the soup thickens slightly to the consistency of single cream (light cream). Gently stir in the flaked fish and heat through without boiling. Ladle into soup plates and serve with the crisp baguette slices spread with aïoli.

PROVENÇAL FISH TERRINE WITH TOMATO VINAIGRETTE

Serves 4

900 G/2 LB MIXED WHITE FISH, SUCH AS MONKFISH (ANGLER FISH), JOHN DORY (PORGY) AND RED MULLET, FILLETED AND SKINNED

225 G/8 OZ LANGOUSTINES OR RAW PRAWNS (SHRIMP)

0.4 G ENVELOPE OF SAFFRON THREADS OR POWDER

5 RIPE TOMATOES

150 ML/¼ PINT/⅔ CUP PROVENÇAL OLIVE OIL

30 ML/2 TBSP BALSAMIC VINEGAR OR SHERRY VINEGAR

SALT AND FRESHLY GROUND BLACK PEPPER

3 MEDIUM LEEKS, TRIMMED

25G/1 OZ/2 TBSP POWDERED GELATINE

60 ML/4 TBSP CHOPPED FRESH BASIL

SPRIGS OF CHERVIL OR BASIL, TO GARNISH

BROTH

1 MEDIUM ONION, PEELED AND SLICED

1 MEDIUM LEEK, TRIMMED AND SLICED

1 CELERY STICK, TRIMMED AND SLICED

1 MEDIUM CARROT, PEELED AND SLICED

1 BOUQUET GARNI AND 6 BLACK PEPPERCORNS

300 ML/½ PINT/1¼ CUPS DRY WHITE WINE

Prepare the fish by removing any stray bones with tweezers and cutting it into large chunks. Shell the langoustines or prawns (shrimp), placing all the shells in a large saucepan. Cover the fish and shellfish and place in the fridge. Soak the saffron in 45 ml/3 tbsp boiling water.

Put all the ingredients for the broth into the pan with the shells. Pour in enough water to cover amply – about 900 ml/1½ pints/4 cups. Slowly bring to the boil, then skim and simmer very gently for 1 hour.

Meanwhile, plunge the tomatoes into boiling water for 10 seconds. Remove with a slotted spoon and plunge them into cold water to stop them overcooking. Slip off the skins, cut out the core, halve lengthways and gently squeeze out the seeds. Slice each half lengthways in two. To make the tomato vinaigrette, place 4 pieces of tomato in a blender with the olive oil and vinegar and purée until smooth. Taste and season with salt and pepper. Set aside.

Strain the broth into another pan, discarding the vegetables, and stir in the saffron infusion. Bring to the boil, add the whole leeks and simmer for 10 minutes or until just tender. Remove the leeks and drain well. Cut them into 2.5 cm/1 inch lengths and set aside to cool.

Bring the broth back to a gentle simmer and add the fish and shellfish. Cook for 1–5 minutes, depending on the fish, until just done. Carefully remove with a slotted spoon and drain on kitchen paper, then leave to cool. Strain the stock

(continued overleaf)

into a measuring jug through a sieve lined with kitchen paper – you should have about 900 ml/1½ pints/4 cups; boil to reduce to this quantity if necessary. Taste and season. Sprinkle the gelatine over the surface of the hot stock and stir until dissolved. Remove from the heat and stir in the chopped basil. Place the jug in an ice bath and leave to cool, stirring occasionally, until syrupy – about 20 minutes. Pour a thin layer into the base of a 1.1-litre/2-pint/5-cup terrine and place in the freezer for a few minutes to set. Carefully mix the fish with the leeks and remaining tomatoes, then place in the terrine. Pour the syrupy jelly over the fish mixture until it covers it completely. Tap the terrine on the work surface to dislodge any trapped air bubbles, then chill for at least 2 hours or until set.

To unmould, dip the terrine briefly in warm water and turn out on to a plate. Serve cut into thick slices, garnished with sprigs of chervil or basil. Either pour a little tomato vinaigrette on each plate or hand it round separately.

RED MULLET WITH BASIL OIL

A pretty dish, at its best using the freshest possible red mullet. I've seen them in Provençal fish markets so fresh that they are still curved, as if just plucked from the sea!

Serves 4

ABOUT 100 ML/4 FL OZ PROVENÇAL OLIVE OIL

40 G/1½ OZ/1 CUP FRESH BASIL LEAVES

SALT AND FRESHLY GROUND BLACK PEPPER

8 RIPE RED TOMATOES

50 G/2 OZ/⅓ CUP BLACK OLIVES, PITTED AND
   ROUGHLY CHOPPED

1 SMALL RED ONION, PEELED AND FINELY CHOPPED

FOUR 350 G/12 OZ RED MULLET, CLEANED AND
   SCALED

SEASONED FLOUR

50 G/2 OZ/½ CUP PINE NUTS

Place 90 ml/6 tbsp of the olive oil in a blender or herb mill with the basil and work until smooth. Season with salt and pepper, pour into a bowl and leave to infuse.

Immerse the tomatoes in boiling water for 10 seconds. Remove with a slotted spoon and plunge into cold water to stop them overcooking. Slip off the skins, halve the tomatoes and squeeze out the seeds. Chop the flesh finely. Mix with the olives and onion and season well, then set aside.

Make 2 diagonal slashes on each side of the red mullet and then dip in seasoned flour, shaking off the excess. Heat an ovenproof skillet or frying pan, big enough to take all the fish, until very hot. Add the remaining olive oil and fry the mullet for 1 minute on each side. Scatter with the pine nuts and immediately transfer to an oven preheated to 190°C/375°F/Gas Mark 5 for 10–12 minutes to finish cooking.

To serve, spoon the tomato and olive salad into the centre of 4 plates. Place a mullet on top, drizzle with the basil oil and cooking juices, and scatter with the pine nuts. Serve immediately.

ROASTED SEA BASS WITH ANCHOVIES AND BASIL

The anchovies melt with the basil and orange into a savoury sauce, which enhances the delicate taste of this fine fish. Roasting on the bone ensures that the fish retains all its flavour. The sea bass should be cleaned very well close to the backbone, otherwise it can taste muddy. Other firm, white-fleshed fish can be cooked in the same manner.

Serves 4

1.2 KG/ 2½ LB SEA BASS, SCALED AND GUTTED

1 ORANGE

50 G/2 OZ/1 PACKED CUP BASIL LEAVES, PLUS EXTRA
TO GARNISH

2 SMALL CANS ANCHOVY FILLETS IN OIL, DRAINED

3 BAY LEAVES

60 ML/4 TBSP PROVENÇAL OLIVE OIL

SALT AND FRESHLY GROUND BLACK PEPPER

Wash the fish inside and out and pat dry on kitchen paper. Make diagonal slashes through the flesh on both sides along the length of the body.

Grate the zest from half the orange. Squeeze the juice from the grated half and slice the remaining half thinly. Pound the basil and anchovies together using a pestle and mortar or in a food processor. Add the grated orange zest and moisten with the orange juice. Use this mixture to fill the slashes in the fish. Lay the fish in an oval ovenproof dish that has been lined with aluminium foil, shiny side up. Fill the cavity with the orange slices and bay leaves, then brush the whole fish with half the oil and season with salt and pepper. Roast uncovered in an oven preheated to 220°C/425°F/Gas Mark 7 for 15 minutes. Baste with any juices and the remaining olive oil and bake for a further 15 minutes. Turn off the oven and leave the fish for 5 minutes to 'set'. Serve immediately, with any juices poured over.

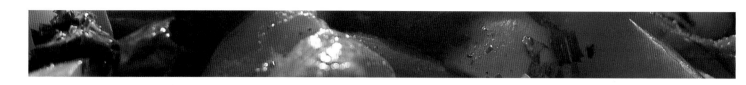

SEARED TUNA NIÇOISE

Fresh tuna seared on a griddle replaces the usual canned variety in this warm robust salad from Nice and the surrounding area. Purists disagree with the inclusion of potatoes, but good waxy potatoes transform the salad into a robust main meal.

Serves 4

TWO 225 G/8 OZ TUNA STEAKS
350 G/12 OZ SMALL WAXY POTATOES
175 G/6 OZ/1½ CUPS FINE GREEN BEANS
3 HARD-BOILED EGGS

2 LARGE RIPE TOMATOES, QUARTERED OR SLICED
SMALL CAN OF ANCHOVY FILLETS, DRAINED
50 G/2 OZ/⅓ CUP BLACK OLIVES

MARINADE

30 ML/2 TBSP LEMON JUICE
75 ML/5 TBSP PROVENÇAL OLIVE OIL

2 GARLIC CLOVES, CRUSHED
SALT AND FRESHLY GROUND BLACK PEPPER

DRESSING

90 ML/6 TBSP EXTRA VIRGIN PROVENÇAL OLIVE OIL
30 ML/2 TBSP WINE VINEGAR OR LEMON JUICE
2 GARLIC CLOVES, CRUSHED
2.5 ML/½ TSP DIJON MUSTARD

30 ML/2 TBSP CAPERS
45 ML/3 TBSP CHOPPED MIXED FRESH HERBS SUCH AS
TARRAGON, CHIVES, BASIL AND CHERVIL

Combine all the ingredients for the marinade in a non-metallic dish. Add the tuna steaks and turn to coat in the marinade, then cover and leave in a cool place for 1 hour. Whisk all the ingredients for the dressing together in a small saucepan, adding salt and pepper to taste, and leave to infuse while you prepare the vegetables.

Boil the potatoes in salted water for 15 minutes or until tender, adding the green beans about 4 minutes before the potatoes are ready. Drain the potatoes and beans. Place the beans in a bowl, slice the potatoes thickly and add to the beans, moistening with a little of the dressing. Peel and quarter the eggs.

Pile the potatoes and beans into a shallow serving dish and arrange the tomatoes and eggs on top. Heat a ridged cast-iron griddle pan or a heavy frying pan (skillet) until smoking. Drain the tuna and sear for 2 minutes on each side. Remove and immediately slice thinly. Pile into the centre of the salad. Finally, scatter over the anchovies and olives, heat the dressing until almost boiling and pour it over the salad. Serve immediately whilst still warm, with crusty bread and lots of chilled Provençal rosé wine.

GRILLED BREAM WITH FENNEL PURÉE

This is a really good way to grill firmer fish and give it that Midi taste, with a delicate purée of slightly aniseedy fennel.

Serves 4

450 G/1 LB FENNEL BULBS, CUT INTO QUARTERS
SQUEEZE OF LEMON JUICE
450 G/1 LB FLOURY POTATOES, PEELED
FOUR 175 G/6 OZ FILLETS OF GOLDEN SEA BREAM
  (PORGY)
60 ML/4 TBSP PROVENÇAL OLIVE OIL, PLUS EXTRA
  FOR BRUSHING

60 ML/4 TBSP TAPENADE (SEE PAGE 85)
SALT AND FRESHLY GROUND BLACK PEPPER
30 ML/2 TBSP CHOPPED FRESH PARSLEY, PLUS EXTRA
  TO GARNISH
10 ML/2 TSP CHOPPED FRESH THYME, PLUS EXTRA TO
  GARNISH
GREEN AND BLACK OLIVES, TO GARNISH

Cook the fennel in boiling salted water with the lemon juice for about 20 minutes or until tender. Cut the potatoes into chunks and cook in a separate pan of boiling salted water for about 20 minutes, until tender.

Meanwhile, slash the skin side of each fish fillet and spread a little tapenade in each cut. Brush with a little olive oil and season with pepper. Place skin side up in a foil-lined grill pan (broiler pan). Heat the grill (broiler).

Drain the fennel and potatoes very well, mash them together, then pass through a sieve or a mouli-légumes. Allow to steam for a few minutes, then gradually beat in the olive oil. Beat in the parsley and thyme and season well with salt and pepper. Keep warm.

Grill (broil) the fish on one side only for about 5 minutes or until cooked.

Place a fillet of bream on a mound of fennel purée on each serving plate with any cooking juices poured over. Garnish with olives, thyme and parsley.

MEAT AND POULTRY

ESTOUFFADE OF LAMB WITH ARTICHOKES

A sweet and delicate stew for spring using tender baby artichokes and waxy new potatoes. Green olives would be a delicious addition to this unusual stew.

Serves 6

1.2KG/2½ LB SHOULDER OF LAMB

45 ML/3 TBSP PROVENÇAL OLIVE OIL

3 ONIONS, PEELED AND FINELY CHOPPED

4 SPRIGS OF FRESH THYME

PIECE OF DRIED ORANGE PEEL (SEE PAGE 100)

SALT AND FRESHLY GROUND BLACK PEPPER

600 ML/1 PINT/2½ CUPS LAMB OR VEGETABLE STOCK

12 FRESH BABY ARTICHOKES OR 12 FROZEN PREPARED ARTICHOKE HEARTS, THAWED

LEMON JUICE

6 MEDIUM-SIZED OR 12 SMALL NEW POTATOES

25 G/1 OZ/2 TBSP BUTTER (OPTIONAL)

15 ML/1 TBSP PLAIN WHITE FLOUR (ALL-PURPOSE FLOUR) (OPTIONAL)

Trim the lamb and cut it into 2.5 cm/1 inch cubes. Heat the oil in a heavy casserole and fry the meat in it in batches until nicely brown. Return all the meat to the pan, then add the onions and cook, stirring well, until beginning to soften. Add the thyme, orange peel, salt and pepper and stock. Bring to the boil, cover and simmer for 1½ hours.

To prepare the fresh artichokes, break off the tough outside leaves, starting at the base, until you expose the central core of pale leaves. Slice off the tough green or purple tips. With a small sharp knife, pare the dark green skin from the base and down the stem. Brush the cut parts with lemon juice to prevent browning. Cut in half and brush with lemon juice again.

If using medium-sized potatoes, cut them into large chunks. Add the potatoes to the casserole with the artichoke hearts and cook for a further 30 minutes. If using frozen or canned artichoke hearts, drain and rinse well and add 5 minutes before the end of cooking. Taste and season. Thicken with a beurre manié, if liked: beat the butter until soft and gradually work in the flour, then whisk this paste into the stew a little at a time. Alternatively, strain off the liquid into a clean pan and boil to reduce, then pour it back over the meat and vegetables.

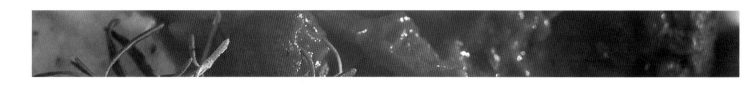

PROVENÇAL RABBIT WITH SOFT ROSEMARY AND GARLIC POLENTA

A country dish combining rabbit with a herb-scented thick tomato sauce and creamy, soft polenta flavoured with garlic and rosemary. Polenta used to be eaten by peasants as a staple food in Provence, as it was nutritious, filling and – unlike this classy version – cheap!

Serves 4

30 ML/2 TBSP OLIVE OIL
4 JOINTS OF RABBIT
1 MEDIUM ONION, PEELED AND CHOPPED
400 G/14 OZ CAN CHOPPED TOMATOES
30 ML/2 TBSP TOMATO PURÉE

150 ML/¼ PINT/⅔ CUP DRY RED WINE
8 SUN-DRIED TOMATOES IN OIL, DRAINED AND SLICED
15 ML/1 TBSP DRIED HERBES DE PROVENCE
SALT AND FRESHLY GROUND BLACK PEPPER
SPRIGS OF FRESH ROSEMARY, TO GARNISH

POLENTA

4 GARLIC CLOVES, PEELED AND CHOPPED
50 G/2 OZ/¼ CUP BUTTER OR OLIVE OIL

45 ML/3 TBSP CHOPPED FRESH ROSEMARY
300 G/11 OZ INSTANT OR QUICK-COOKING POLENTA

Heat the oil in a medium saucepan and brown the rabbit joints. Add the onion and cook for 5 minutes, until the onion is soft and golden. Add the tomatoes, tomato purée and wine. Bring to the boil, then add the sun-dried tomatoes and dried herbs. Simmer for 30 minutes or until the sauce is well reduced and the rabbit is tender, stirring occasionally. Season to taste.

Meanwhile, make the polenta. Bring 1.4 litres/2½ pints/6 cups water to the boil with 10 ml/2 tsp salt. Fry the garlic in the butter or oil until golden, then stir in the rosemary and set aside. Sprinkle the polenta into the boiling water in a continuous shower, stirring or whisking to prevent lumps forming. Beat in the garlic and rosemary mixture and simmer for 5–10 minutes, stirring constantly, until thickened to the consistency of soft mashed potato. Season well with salt and pepper.

Spoon the polenta into 4 large soup plates and make a dip in the centre of each one. Place a piece of rabbit on each serving and spoon over the tomato sauce, then garnish with sprigs of rosemary.

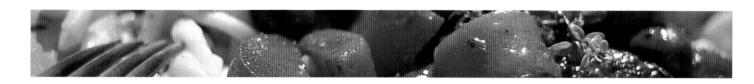

DAUBE DE BOEUF NIÇOISE

A covered casserole dish called a daubière gave its name to this famous beef and wine stew.

Serves 6

1.4 KG/3 LB STEWING BEEF

45 ML/3 TBSP OLIVE OIL

125 G/4 OZ PIECE UNSMOKED BACON, CUT INTO
LARDONS (SMALL DICE)

2 MEDIUM ONIONS, PEELED AND QUARTERED

2 MEDIUM CARROTS, PEELED AND ROUGHLY CHOPPED

SMALL PIECE OF DRIED ORANGE PEEL (SEE PAGE 100)

3 GARLIC CLOVES, PEELED AND LIGHTLY BRUISED

45 ML/3 TBSP MARC OR BRANDY

30 ML/2 TBSP TOMATO PURÉE OR SUN-DRIED
TOMATO PASTE (SEE PAGE 101)

15 ML/1 TBSP DRIED HERBES DE PROVENCE

ABOUT 600 ML/1 PINT/2½ CUPS BEEF STOCK

125 G/4 OZ/⅔ CUP SMALL BLACK NIÇOISE OLIVES

SALT AND FRESHLY GROUND BLACK PEPPER

CHOPPED FRESH PARSLEY, TO GARNISH

MARINADE

2 BOTTLES OF RED WINE

3 ONIONS, PEELED AND ROUGHLY CHOPPED

2 GARLIC CLOVES, PEELED AND LIGHTLY BRUISED

2 CARROTS, PEELED AND CHOPPED

1 CELERY STICK, TRIMMED AND CHOPPED

2 BAY LEAVES PLUS 2 LARGE SPRIGS OF THYME

8 PEPPERCORNS, CRUSHED

2 CLOVES

For the marinade, pour the wine into a large saucepan or sauté pan and bring to the boil. Boil hard until reduced by half. Add all remaining marinade ingredients and stir well. Remove from the heat and leave to cool completely. Trim the meat of any fat or gristle and cut it into 6.5 cm/2½ inch pieces. Place in a large plastic bag with the cold marinade. Shake the bag to mix, then seal and place in the fridge to marinate overnight. Next day, open the bag and pour the contents into a colander set over a bowl to catch the liquid. Remove the meat and pat dry. Discard the vegetables. Heat the oil in a large flameproof casserole and brown the lardons. Transfer to a plate, then brown the beef well in batches. Transfer the meat to a plate. Brown the onions and carrots in the same way. Return the bacon and beef to the casserole with the vegetables and tuck in the orange peel and garlic cloves. Pour over the reserved marinade and the marc or brandy, then stir in the tomato purée or paste and herbs. Add enough stock to cover the meat and vegetables, then stir in the olives and season well. Bring to the boil, turn down the heat, cover tightly and simmer gently for 2 hours or until the meat is very tender. Top the liquid up with extra stock if it evaporates too quickly.

Cool then place in the fridge overnight. Next day, skim off the fat and remove the orange peel before reheating.

GARLIC CHICKEN

This chicken is roasted with an immense amount of garlic, which becomes sweet and nutty when cooked in this way. A chicken brick is very good in this recipe as it keeps in all the flavour.

Serves 6

1.8 KG/4 LB FREE-RANGE CHICKEN

1 LEMON

2 SPRIGS OF FRESH ROSEMARY

2 SPRIGS OF FRESH THYME

4 LARGE HEADS OF GARLIC

150 ML/¼ PINT/⅔ CUP PROVENÇAL OLIVE OIL

SALT AND FRESHLY GROUND BLACK PEPPER

Put the chicken in a large shallow roasting dish. Cut the lemon in half and squeeze one half over the chicken. Tuck both lemon halves inside the chicken cavity with the rosemary and thyme. Peel the very outer skin away from the garlic and slice the heads of garlic horizontally in half, placing 2 halves in the cavity of the bird with the lemon and herbs. Rub the bird with a little of the olive oil and season with salt and pepper. Roast in an oven preheated to 180°C/350°F/Gas Mark 4 for 1½ hours, basting occasionally.

Place the remaining halved garlic heads cut-side up around the chicken 30 minutes before it is ready and baste with the remaining olive oil. After 30 minutes the garlic should be soft – remove from the dish and keep warm.

Turn the oven up to 220°C/425°F/Gas Mark 7 for 5–10 minutes to crisp the chicken skin. Serve the chicken surrounded by the roasted garlic with the pan juices to pour over the meat when carved. The soft garlic cloves can be prised out of their husks with a fork and mashed on to the chicken as you eat it.

PARTRIDGE WITH LENTILS

A heartwarming dish for a winter's day.

Serves 4

50 G/2 OZ/¼ CUP BUTTER
4 PARTRIDGES
225 G/8 OZ PICKLING ONIONS, PEELED
2 CARROTS, PEELED AND CHOPPED

150 ML/¼ PINT/⅔ CUP DRY WHITE WINE
600 ML/1 PINT/2½ CUPS CHICKEN STOCK
4 LARGE SPRIGS OF FRESH THYME
SALT AND FRESHLY GROUND BLACK PEPPER

LENTILS

225 G/8 OZ/1¼ CUPS BROWN OR GREEN LENTILS
30 ML/2 TBSP PROVENÇAL OLIVE OIL
1 SMALL ONION, PEELED AND FINELY CHOPPED

1 SMALL CARROT, PEELED AND FINELY CHOPPED
1 GARLIC CLOVE, PEELED AND FINELY CHOPPED
450 ML/¾ PINT/2 CUPS CHICKEN STOCK

Soak the lentils in hot water to cover for 1 hour. Meanwhile, melt the butter in a flameproof casserole and brown the birds well on all sides. Transfer to a plate and add the pickling onions and carrots to the casserole. Brown these well and return the partridges to the pan. Pour in the wine and boil until reduced by half. Add the stock and thyme and season well. Bring to the boil, cover tightly and simmer gently for 2 hours, until the birds are tender.

Drain the soaked lentils. Heat the oil in a saucepan and brown the onion, carrot and garlic. Stir in the lentils, then pour in the stock. Season well, bring to the boil and simmer, covered, for 25–30 minutes or until just tender. Top up with extra stock if looking dry.

When the partridges are cooked, remove the thyme, lift out the birds and place in a warm serving dish. Spoon the lentils into the casserole and mix well. Reheat, taste and season and spoon around the birds.

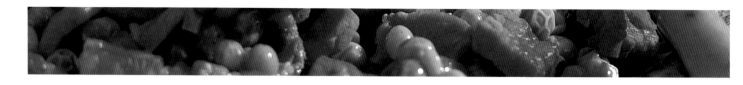

SQUAB BRAISED WITH PEAS AND COUNTRY HAM

This classic game dish from the hills of Provence is just as good made with pigeon or poussin. Fresh tender young peas give a sweet earthiness to the juicy flesh of the squab. Use Italian prosciutto if raw French country ham is difficult to find.

Serves 4

50 G/2 OZ/¼ CUP BUTTER

4 SQUAB, PIGEONS OR POUSSINS

1 LARGE ONION, PEELED AND FINELY CHOPPED

125 G/4 OZ PIECE OF JAMBON CRU DE PAYS (FRENCH RAW COUNTRY HAM), CHOPPED

6 GARLIC CLOVES, PEELED

150 ML/¼ PINT/⅔ CUP WHITE WINE

450 ML/¾ PINT/2 CUPS CHICKEN STOCK

2 SPRIGS OF FRESH THYME

15 ML/1 TBSP PLAIN WHITE FLOUR (ALL-PURPOSE FLOUR)

BUTTER AND OIL FOR FRYING

4 SLICES OF WHITE BREAD

450 G/1 LB FRESH SHELLED PEAS

SALT AND FRESHLY GROUND BLACK PEPPER

Melt half the butter in a large saucepan and brown the birds all over. Transfer to a plate. Add the onion and chopped ham to the pan and cook over a high heat until begining to brown. Add the whole garlic cloves, wine, stock and thyme and bring to the boil. Replace the birds, cover tightly and simmer for 45 minutes or until the birds are almost cooked through.

Beat the remaining butter until soft and gradually work in the flour to make a beurre manié. Set aside. Heat a little oil and butter in a frying pan (skillet) and fry the bread on both sides until golden brown. Drain well and keep warm. Add the peas to the birds and simmer uncovered for another 10 minutes, until the peas are tender but still firm. Remove the birds and the garlic cloves from the pan and keep warm. Whisk the beurre manié, a little piece at a time, into the peas and sauce. Bring to the boil and simmer for 5 minutes until slightly thickened and glossy, then return the birds to the sauce. Taste and season. Place a bread croute on each serving plate and mash the whole cloves of garlic on each croute. Place a bird on top, spoon the pea and bacon sauce around and serve immediately.

VEGETABLES AND SALADS

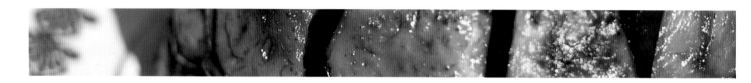

PAPETON D'AUBERGINES

A mousse of puréed aubergines (eggplant) created in Avignon by a 14th-century Papal chef. The mould is lined with sliced fried aubergine, the whole being turned out to serve.

Serves 6

5 LARGE AUBERGINES (EGGPLANT), ABOUT
1.5 KG/3¼ LB IN TOTAL
SALT AND FRESHLY GROUND BLACK PEPPER
PROVENÇAL OLIVE OIL FOR FRYING
3 GARLIC CLOVES, PEELED AND CRUSHED

2 ONIONS, PEELED AND FINELY CHOPPED
6 EGGS
LARGE BUNCH OF PARSLEY, CHOPPED
FRESHLY GRATED NUTMEG
5 ML/1 TSP CHOPPED FRESH THYME

Cut 3 of the aubergines (eggplant) into small cubes. Cut the remaining ones into slices 1.25 cm/½ inch thick and set aside. Place the cubed aubergine (eggplant) in a colander and sprinkle with salt. Leave to stand for 30 minutes to draw out the bitter juices, then rinse and drain well.

Heat 45 ml/3 tbsp of oil in a saucepan and add the garlic, onions and cubed aubergine (eggplant). Cook slowly for 30 minutes, stirring from time to time, until completely tender.

Pour some olive oil into a large frying pan (skillet) to give a depth of 1.25 cm/½ inch. When it is very hot, add the sliced aubergine (eggplant) and fry in batches over a fairly high heat until brown. Drain on kitchen paper and use to line a 1.7-litre/3-pint/7–8-cup straight-sided dish such as a soufflé dish or charlotte mould.

Place the cooked cubed aubergine (eggplant) mixture in a food processor with the eggs, parsley, nutmeg, thyme and salt and pepper and blend until smooth. Ladle into the lined dish and smooth the surface. Set in a roasting tin (roasting pan) of hot water and bake in an oven preheated to 180°C/350°F/Gas Mark 4 for about 40 minutes or until the mixture is firm to the touch and a knife inserted in the centre comes out clean. Remove from the roasting tin (roasting pan) and leave for 10 minutes before turning out on to a warm serving plate.

TIAN DE COURGETTES

This makes a good light lunch dish or an accompaniment to fish or meat. A tian is a large shallow earthenware dish, often used for cooking vegetable dishes.

Serves 4

900 G/2 LB MEDIUM COURGETTES (ZUCCHINI), THINLY SLICED

125 G/4 OZ/½ CUP LONG GRAIN RICE

SALT AND FRESHLY GROUND BLACK PEPPER

ABOUT 450 ML/¾ PINT/2 CUPS HOT VEGETABLE OR CHICKEN STOCK

75 G/3 OZ/¾ CUP GRUYÈRE CHEESE, GRATED

Oil a tian or similar shallow dish. Arrange the courgettes (zucchini) in it in layers, sprinkling with rice and salt and pepper between each layer and ending in a layer of courgettes (zucchini).

Pour in enough hot stock to come up to the top layer. Cover with aluminium foil and bake in an oven preheated to 170°C/325°F/Gas Mark 3 for 1 hour. Uncover and sprinkle with the cheese. Grill (broil) until golden and bubbling, then serve immediately.

HARICOTS VERTS NIÇOIS

This is one of the great 'little dishes' of Provence – green beans in a rich tomato sauce, served hot or cold. Leeks, onions and many other vegetables can be cooked in the same way.

Serves 4

450 G/1 LB GREEN BEANS OR RUNNER BEANS, TRIMMED

3 RIPE RED TOMATOES

30 ML/2 TBSP PROVENÇAL OLIVE OIL

1 GARLIC CLOVE, PEELED AND CHOPPED

SALT AND FRESHLY GROUND BLACK PEPPER

CHOPPED FRESH PARSLEY, TO GARNISH

Blanch the beans in boiling salted water for 3 minutes, then drain and refresh under cold running water. Plunge the tomatoes into boiling water for 10 seconds. Drain and refresh in cold water, then slip off the skins. Chop the tomatoes roughly. Heat the oil in a pan and add the beans, tomatoes and garlic. Cook gently for 10 minutes or until the tomatoes have completely melted. Taste and season. Serve warm or cold, sprinkled with the parsley.

COUSCOUS SALAD

The North African influence is very strong in the cooking of Provence – try this new way of serving couscous, prepared like tabbouleh.

Serves 6

450 G/1 LB/2⅔ CUPS COUSCOUS

SALT AND FRESHLY GROUND BLACK PEPPER

1 CUCUMBER

5 ML/1 TSP HARISSA (SEE PAGE 105)

50 G/2 OZ/1 PACKED CUP CHOPPED MIXED FRESH

BASIL, MINT AND PARSLEY

45 ML/3 TBSP PROVENÇAL OLIVE OIL

6 SPRING ONIONS (SCALLIONS), TRIMMED AND

CHOPPED

225 G/8 OZ CHERRY TOMATOES, HALVED

LEMON JUICE, TO TASTE

SALT AND FRESHLY GROUND BLACK PEPPER

Put the couscous into a bowl and pour 450 ml/¾ pint/2 cups boiling water over it. Stir, cover and leave to swell for 30 minutes.

Halve the cucumber lengthways and scoop out the seeds. Dice very finely. Fluff up the couscous with 2 forks to remove any lumps. Stir in the harissa, herbs and olive oil, then the cucumber, spring onions (scallions) and cherry tomatoes. Season with lemon juice, salt and pepper. The salad should be very green, quite fiery and lemony. Pile into a dish and serve.

PROVENÇAL STUFFED VEGETABLES

A glorious show of the variety of vegetables in the market, making a meal on their own with good crusty bread. If you can find red Camargue rice, use it in this recipe for its good colour and nutty flavour. Otherwise use brown or white long grain rice.

Serves 2–4

1 MEDIUM AUBERGINE (EGGPLANT)
1 LARGE (BELL) PEPPER
OLIVE OIL FOR BRUSHING

2 LARGE BEEF TOMATOES
2 MEDIUM COURGETTES (ZUCCHINI)

STUFFING

30 ML (2 TBSP) PROVENÇAL OLIVE OIL
1 ONION, PEELED AND CHOPPED
2 GARLIC CLOVES, PEELED AND CHOPPED
450 G/1 LB/4 CUPS COOKED RICE

50 G/2 OZ/½ CUP PINE NUTS, TOASTED
30 ML/2 TBSP RAISINS
30 ML/2 TBSP CHOPPED FRESH BASIL
SALT AND FRESHLY GROUND BLACK PEPPER

To make the stuffing, heat the olive oil in a saucepan and add the onion and garlic. Cook over a gentle heat for about 10 minutes, until soft and golden. Stir in the rice, pine nuts, raisins, basil, salt and pepper. Set aside.

Halve the aubergine (eggplant) lengthways and scoop out a channel in each half. Cut the pepper horizontally in half and scoop out the seeds. Stand each half like a cup on a baking sheet with the aubergines (eggplant). Brush with oil and bake in an oven preheated to 180°C/350°F/Gas Mark 4 for 15–20 minutes, until softened. Remove from the oven and set aside to cool.

Cut the tops off the tomatoes and scoop out the seeds. Halve the courgettes (zucchini) lengthways and scoop out a channel in each half. Set all the vegetables on a baking sheet and fill with the stuffing, then drizzle with olive oil. Place the tops on the tomatoes. Bake the vegetables for 25 minutes or until soft and tender. Serve warm or cold.

BABY ARTICHOKES À LA BARIGOULE

An ancient Provençal dish of artichokes stewed simply in olive oil – nothing else is necessary.

Serves 4

12 FRESH BABY ARTICHOKES
LEMON JUICE

300 ML/½ PINT/1¼ CUPS PROVENÇAL OLIVE OIL
SALT

To prepare the artichokes, trim the stalks to about 1.25 cm/½ inch long. Break off the tough outside leaves, starting at the base, until you expose a central core of pale leaves. Slice off the tough green or purple tips. With a small sharp knife, pare the dark green skin from the base and down the stem. Brush the cut parts of the artichokes with lemon juice to prevent browning.

Place the artichokes in an even layer in a saucepan and pour in the olive oil, then add enough water to cover the artichokes completely. Bring to a rapid boil and continue to boil for 15–20 minutes (they will splutter) until all the water evaporates and the artichokes start to fry. The artichokes will turn golden brown and the leaves will spread out like petals. Serve with a little of the oil poured over and sprinkled with a little salt.

TOMATOES BAKED WITH A GARLIC CRUST

An easy version of the classic stuffed tomato, using small tomatoes baked under a crust of chopped garlic, toasted breadcrumbs and olive oil. This makes a simple and delicious accompaniment to chicken or fish dishes.

Serves 6

6 SLICES OF STALE BREAD

SMALL CAN OF ANCHOVY FILLETS IN OIL, DRAINED

6 GARLIC CLOVES, PEELED AND CHOPPED

45 ML/3 TBSP CHOPPED FRESH PARSLEY

EXTRA PARSLEY, TO SERVE

SALT AND FRESHLY GROUND BLACK PEPPER

700 G/1½ LB SMALL PLUM TOMATOES

PROVENÇAL OLIVE OIL FOR DRIZZLING

Tear up the bread, place in a food processor with the anchovies and blend until it turns to crumbs. Spoon into a frying pan and dry fry until golden. Remove from the heat. Stir the garlic into the crumbs with the parsley, salt and freshly ground black pepper.

Halve the tomatoes around the middle and place, cut-side up, close together in a single layer in a shallow ovenproof dish. Sprinkle the breadcrumb and anchovy mixture evenly over the tomatoes and drizzle well with olive oil.

Bake in an oven preheated to 220°C/425°F/Gas Mark 7 for about 20 minutes, until the crust is golden and the tomatoes are soft. The tomatoes will slightly disintegrate under the crust. Scatter with more parsley to serve.

ROASTED SUMMER VEGETABLES

This colourful mix of roasted, caramelized vegetables makes a delicious accompaniment to poultry and fish. Served cold or at room temperature it also makes a superb salad. Experiment with other vegetables, such as aubergines (eggplant) and baby artichokes.

Serves 6

2 MEDIUM ONIONS

2 MEDIUM SWEET RED PEPPERS

3 COURGETTES (ZUCCHINI) OR SMALL ROUND SQUASH

150 ML/¼ PINT/⅔ CUP PROVENÇAL OLIVE OIL

3 LARGE HEADS OF GARLIC

4 SPRIGS OF FRESH THYME

COARSE SALT AND FRESHLY GROUND BLACK PEPPER

ROUGHLY CHOPPED FRESH PARSLEY, TO SERVE

Halve the onions through the root, leaving the root intact. Peel them and cut each half in 2 lengthways to give 8 pieces. Halve and seed the peppers, removing the stalks and any white membrane. Cut each pepper into quarters. Halve or quarter the courgettes (zucchini) or squash. Place all these vegetables in a roasting tin (roasting pan), pour over the olive oil and toss well. Cut the whole heads of garlic horizontally in half and place cut-side down amongst the vegetables. Roast in an oven preheated to 200°C/400°F/Gas Mark 6 for about 35 minutes, turning the vegetables twice and adding the thyme sprigs about 10 minutes before the vegetables are ready. They should be tender and starting to brown but not disintegrating. The garlic should be golden and soft.

Season well with salt and pepper and turn into a warm serving dish. Sprinkle with chopped parsley to serve.

SAUCES AND SPREADS

AÏOLI

This classic, golden garlic mayonnaise can be served as a main dish with a variety of cooked vegetables, as a dip with drinks, or used as a sauce to stir into soups. You can make it in a pestle and mortar in the traditional way but it is almost foolproof in a food processor!

Makes about	8 LARGE GARLIC CLOVES, PEELED AND ROUGHLY	SALT
500 ml/18 fl oz/	CHOPPED	ABOUT 450 ML/¾ PINT/2 CUPS PROVENÇAL OLIVE OIL
2¼ cups	2 EGG YOLKS	LEMON JUICE

All the ingredients must be at room temperature. Place the garlic, egg yolks and a pinch of salt in a food processor and blend until very smooth. With the machine running, pour in the oil in a thin, steady stream until you have added about half and the mixture starts to thicken. Add a squeeze of lemon juice and then pour in the oil more boldly until it is all used up and the aïoli is like a thick ointment. Taste and check the seasoning, adding more lemon juice if you like. It should be singing with garlic! Set aside in a cool place – but not in the refrigerator, as it may split.

To make the aïoli by hand, crush the garlic with the salt in a pestle and mortar until creamy, then stir in the egg yolks. Using a whisk, add the oil drop by drop, whisking well between additions, until it begins to emulsify with the egg. Continue doing this very slowly until you have added half the oil and the mixture starts to thicken. Whisk in a little lemon juice, then add the oil more boldly (by tablespoons), again whisking well between additions to emulsify the oil, until it is all used up.

The more oil you use, the thicker the aïoli will be. Stir in a little hot water or milk for a thinner sauce, or start with more egg yolk for a more eggy taste.

OVERLEAF: TAPENADE. AÏOLI AND ANCHOÏADE

TAPENADE

The name tapenade comes from the Provençal word tapena, meaning capers, and describes a thick sauce or spread made from garlic, capers and anchovies. This recipe adds rich dark olives and charred sweet peppers for a more intense, almost smoky flavour. It is delicious with eggs in any form, especially hard-boiled, tossed with new potatoes or pasta, or spread on grilled bread.

Serves about 10

1 SMALL SWEET RED PEPPER

3 GARLIC CLOVES, UNPEELED

225 G/8 OZ/1⅓ CUPS BLACK OLIVES, PREFERABLY WRINKLY GREEK-STYLE ONES, PITTED

30–45 ML/2–3 TBSP SALTED CAPERS OR CAPERS IN VINEGAR, RINSED

12 ANCHOVY FILLETS OR 1 SMALL CAN TUNA FISH IN OIL, DRAINED

ABOUT 150 ML/¼ PINT/⅔ CUP PROVENÇAL OLIVE OIL

LEMON JUICE

FRESHLY GROUND BLACK PEPPER

45 ML/3 TBSP CHOPPED FRESH BASIL (OPTIONAL)

Place the red pepper and garlic cloves under a hot grill (broiler) and grill (broil) for about 15 minutes, turning until completely charred all over. Leave to cool, then rub the skin off the pepper (do not wash) and remove the stalk and seeds. Peel the skin off the garlic.

Place the pepper, garlic, olives, capers and anchovies or tuna fish in a food processor and process until roughly chopped. With the machine running, slowly add the olive oil until you have a fairly smooth, dark paste. Season with lemon juice and black pepper, then stir in the basil, if using.

Store in the fridge in a jar, covered with a layer of olive oil to exclude the air, for up to 1 month.

ANCHOÏADE

A strong, savoury anchovy paste, essential to Provençal cuisine, which is spread on toasted bread and heated in the oven. It is also very good stirred into tomato sauces to give them a subtle 'kick', and quite delicious mixed with creamy fresh goat's cheese and spread on crusty bread.

Makes about
225 g/8 oz/
I cup

3 SMALL CANS ANCHOVY FILLETS IN OIL

2 GARLIC CLOVES, PEELED AND ROUGHLY CHOPPED

30 ML/2 TBSP PINE NUTS OR GROUND ALMONDS

15 ML/1 TBSP SHERRY VINEGAR OR 5ML/1 TSP
  BALSAMIC VINEGAR

ABOUT 60 ML/4 TBSP PROVENÇAL OLIVE OIL

FRESHLY GROUND BLACK PEPPER

Drain the anchovies and pat dry on kitchen paper. Place them in a food processor with the garlic and pine nuts or ground almonds and blend until a paste is formed. Add the vinegar and, with the machine running, slowly pour in the olive oil until it has all been absorbed and the mixture has a thick, pastelike consistency. Taste and season with black pepper, and more vinegar if you like.

To make anchoïade with a pestle and mortar, pound the anchovies and garlic together until creamy. Add the pine nuts or almonds and pound until amalgamated. Stir in the vinegar, then beat the olive oil into the mixture drop by drop until you have a smooth paste. Check the seasoning.

Use straight away as a spread or dip, or stir into mayonnaise if you prefer a milder flavour. To store, spoon into a jar and cover the surface with olive oil. Keep in the refrigerator for up to 1 month.

ROUILLE

This fiery, rust-coloured sauce was traditionally made with very simple ingredients, such as garlic, red chillies, soaked bread, olive oil and fish broth, to serve with fish soups. However, this version is a little more substantial, more of a dip or spread. It can of course still be whisked into fish soups like its predecessor.

Makes about 300 ml/½ pint/ 1¼ cups

1 SMALL SWEET RED PEPPER
2 SMALL SLICES OF STALE BREAD
A LITTLE MILK OR FISH STOCK
3 GARLIC CLOVES, PEELED
1.25 ML/¼ TSP SALT

10 ML/2 TSP HARISSA (SEE PAGE 105) OR 2 SMALL RED CHILLIES, SEEDED
0.4 G ENVELOPE OF SAFFRON THREADS OR POWDER
3 HARD-BOILED EGG YOLKS
ABOUT 150 ML/¼ PINT/⅔ CUP PROVENÇAL OLIVE OIL

Place the sweet red pepper under a hot grill (broiler) and grill (broil) for about 15 minutes, turning until completely charred all over. Place in a plastic bag, seal and leave to steam for 10 minutes.

Meanwhile, soak the bread in a little milk or fish stock and squeeze dry. Place the bread, garlic, salt, harissa or chillies, saffron and egg yolks in a small blender or food processor. Peel the skin off the pepper, discarding the stalk and seeds, then add the flesh to the food processor. Blend until smooth.

With the machine still running, add the oil in a thin steady stream until the sauce thickens like mayonnaise. The more oil you add the thicker it will become – adding too much will make it split, so be careful. Taste and season. Keep, covered, in the refrigerator but bring to room temperature before serving.

CHICK PEA, HARICOT BEAN AND GARLIC PURÉE

A delightful purée to spread on toasted country bread or use as a dip, inspired by the Provençal love of Arab ingredients, especially chick peas. Despite the large quantity of garlic in the mixture, it tastes quite subtle and nutty.

Makes about 600 ml/1 pint/ 2½ cups

125 G/4 OZ/⅔ CUP DRIED HARICOT BEANS (NAVY BEANS)

125 G/4 OZ/⅔ CUP DRIED CHICK PEAS

6 LARGE GARLIC CLOVES, PEELED

1 BAY LEAF

A FEW SPRIGS OF FRESH THYME

PINCH OF BICARBONATE OF SODA (BAKING SODA)

60 ML/4 TBSP PROVENÇAL OLIVE OIL

SALT AND FRESHLY GROUND BLACK PEPPER

60 ML/4 TBSP CHOPPED FRESH PARSLEY, OR HALF PARSLEY, HALF BASIL

Wash the dried beans and peas very well, then place in a saucepan and cover with plenty of cold water. Leave to soak overnight. The next day, drain well, return to the pan and cover with cold water. Add half the garlic, plus the bay leaf, thyme and bicarbonate of soda (baking soda), and bring to the boil. Half cover and simmer until soft – about 45 minutes–1 hour, depending on the age of the beans. Drain over a bowl to catch the cooking liquid and remove the herbs. Place the beans in a food processor and process with a ladleful of the cooking liquid to start. Add more liquid until you have a very soft consistency, like mashed potatoes.

Finely chop the remaining garlic. Heat the oil in a large non-stick frying pan (skillet), add the garlic and cook until golden. Stir in the bean purée and cook over a moderate heat for about 10 minutes, stirring all the time, until the mixture begins to darken a little and thicken to a stiff paste. Taste and season well with salt and pepper, then beat in the chopped herbs. Leave to cool, then cover and refrigerate. Serve at room temperature.

NOTE

Extra olive oil or warm milk can be beaten into the purée while it is still warm to give a softer result.

COULIS DE TOMATES

This rich fresh tomato sauce is the basis of many Provençal dishes. Be sure to use very ripe tomatoes – hard British ones are only for salads. Italian plum tomatoes are good if really ripe, as they do not hold much water and are very sweet. Alternatively use bottled crushed tomatoes, not canned whole tomatoes, which are too watery. If the sauce is still not rich enough when cooked, add some Sun-dried Tomato Paste (see page 101) and simmer for another 15 minutes.

Makes about 600 ml/1 pint/ 2½ cups

900 G/2 LB RIPE RED TOMATOES

75 ML/5 TBSP PROVENÇAL OLIVE OIL

225 G/8 OZ MILD, SWEET ONIONS, PEELED AND SLICED

6 GARLIC CLOVES, PEELED AND CRUSHED

3 LARGE SPRIGS OF FRESH THYME

2 BAY LEAVES

SALT

Remove the core from the tomatoes with a small sharp knife. Plunge the tomatoes into boiling water for 5–10 seconds, remove and refresh in cold water. Slip off the skins. Cut in half around the middle and gently squeeze out the seeds. Heat the olive oil in a large sauté pan, add the onions and garlic and cook slowly for at least 20 minutes, until soft and golden. Add the tomatoes and herbs. Turn up the heat and stir gently to help the tomatoes cook and break up. Simmer gently for 1 hour, stirring occasionally to prevent sticking, until the mixture has thickened and the oil is beginning to separate. Remove the herbs and purée the sauce in a blender or food processor. Taste and season. If not using immediately, leave to cool, then transfer to a bowl and cover with a layer of olive oil before refrigerating. It will keep in the fridge for 2 weeks. Alternatively make a large batch and freeze it.

DESSERTS

CHERRY CLAFOUTIS

The Provençal version of this dessert uses a type of sponge rather than a batter, not unlike the English Bakewell tart, and is studded with juicy cherries.

Serves 6

PASTRY

225 G/8 OZ/2 CUPS PLAIN WHITE FLOUR (ALL-PURPOSE FLOUR)

30 ML/2 TBSP ICING SUGAR (CONFECTIONERS' SUGAR)

125 G/4 OZ/ ½ CUP BUTTER

2 EGG YOLKS

FILLING

2 EGGS

50 G/2 OZ/¼ CUP SUGAR

60 ML/4 TBSP DOUBLE CREAM (HEAVY CREAM)

45 ML/3 TBSP GROUND ALMONDS

15 ML/1 TBSP KIRSCH

25 G/1 OZ/2 TBSP MELTED BUTTER

225 G/8 OZ RIPE CHERRIES, PITTED

ICING SUGAR (CONFECTIONERS' SUGAR), FOR DUSTING

To make the pastry, sift the flour and sugar into a bowl and rub in the butter. Stir in the egg yolks and enough iced water to bind to a firm dough. Knead lightly until smooth, then wrap in cling film (plastic wrap) and chill for 30 minutes. Use to line six 10-cm/4-inch tartlet tins (tart pans) and chill for 30 minutes again.

For the filling, lightly whisk together the eggs, sugar and cream. Stir in the ground almonds, Kirsch and melted butter. Arrange the cherries in the uncooked tartlets and pour over the filling. Bake in an oven preheated to 200°C/400°F/Gas Mark 6 for 15–20 minutes, until golden. Serve warm, dusted with icing sugar (confectioners' sugar) and accompanied by crème fraîche, if liked.

NOTE

You could make this in a 25-cm/10-inch flan tin (tart pan), in which case the pastry should be baked blind before the filling is added.

HONEY AND WALNUT TART WITH CRÈME ANGLAISE

This is a very sweet and aromatic tart, to be served in small slices.

Serves 6–8 **PASTRY**	225 G/8 OZ/2 CUPS PLAIN WHITE FLOUR (ALL-PURPOSE FLOUR) 30 ML/2 TBSP ICING SUGAR (CONFECTIONERS' SUGAR)	125 G/4 OZ/½ CUP BUTTER 2 EGG YOLKS
FILLING	125 G/4 OZ/½ CUP UNSALTED BUTTER, SOFTENED 125 G/4 OZ/½ CUP LIGHT SOFT BROWN SUGAR 3 EGGS 15 ML/1 TBSP ORANGE FLOWER WATER	175 G/6 OZ /¾ CUP LAVENDER HONEY 225 G/8 OZ/2 CUPS SHELLED WALNUT PIECES SALT
CRÈME ANGLAISE	1 VANILLA POD (VANILLA BEAN) 300 ML/½ PINT/1¼ CUPS MILK 15 ML/1 TBSP CASTER SUGAR (SUPERFINE SUGAR)	2 EGG YOLKS 30 ML/2 TBSP COGNAC OR ARMAGNAC

To make the pastry, sift the flour and sugar into a bowl and rub in the butter. Stir in the egg yolks and enough iced water to bind to a firm dough. Knead lightly until smooth, then wrap in cling film (plastic wrap) and chill for 30 minutes. Use to line a 23-cm/9-inch fluted flan tin (tart pan). Chill for 30 minutes, then bake blind for 15–20 minutes in an oven preheated to 375°F/190°C/Gas Mark 5.

To make the filling, cream the butter and sugar together until light and fluffy. Gradually beat in the eggs, one at a time, then beat in the orange flower water. Heat the honey in a small pan until runny but not very hot. Stir it into the butter mixture with the walnuts and a pinch of salt. Pour into the pastry case and bake for 45 minutes at 180°C/350°F/Gas Mark 4, until lightly browned and risen. The filling will sink a little on cooling.

To make the crème anglaise, split the vanilla pod (vanilla bean) open with a sharp knife and place in a saucepan with the milk and sugar. Bring almost to the boil and then remove from the heat and leave to infuse for 15 minutes. Remove the vanilla pod (vanilla bean). Beat the egg yolks in a bowl and pour on the hot milk, stirring all the time. Return to the pan and stir with a wooden spoon over a gentle heat until the custard thickens enough to coat the back of the spoon. Pour into a cold bowl and stir in the cognac or Armagnac. Cover with cling film (plastic wrap), cool and chill.

Serve the tart warm or cold, with the crème anglaise.

MARRON GLACÉ ICE CREAM

Provence is the magical land of candied fruits, marrons glacés being one of the most famous and treasured delicacies of the region. Here a smooth sweet chestnut ice cream is studded with chunks of marron glacé.

Serves 6

75 G/3 OZ/⅓ CUP CASTER SUGAR (SUPERFINE SUGAR)

2 EGGS, SEPARATED

200 G/7 OZ CAN CRÈME DE MARRONS (SWEETENED CHESTNUT PURÉE)

300 ML/½ PINT/1¼ CUPS DOUBLE CREAM (HEAVY CREAM)

6 MARRONS GLACÉS (CANDIED CHESTNUTS), CUT INTO CHUNKS, PLUS EXTRA TO DECORATE

Line a 1.1-litre/2-pint/5-cup loaf tin (bread pan) with cling film (plastic wrap), letting it overlap the sides. Put the sugar in a saucepan with 60 ml/4 tbsp water and heat very gently until the sugar has dissolved. Bring to the boil and boil until the syrup reaches a temperature of 110°C/230°F on a sugar thermometer (candy thermometer). Meanwhile whisk the egg whites in a large bowl until stiff but not dry. Slowly pour the sugar syrup on to the egg whites, whisking all the time – an electric beater is useful for this. The whites will become thick and meringue-like. In another bowl, beat the egg yolks until pale and creamy, then beat in the crème de marrons (chestnut purée). Whisk the cream until it just holds its shape. Fold the meringue mixture into the chestnut mixture, then fold in the cream. Stir in the chopped chestnuts. Turn the mixture into the prepared loaf tin (bread pan) and freeze for at least 3 hours or until it is quite firm.

Turn out the ice cream, remove the cling film (plastic wrap) and slice with a hot knife. Serve decorated with extra marrons glacés.

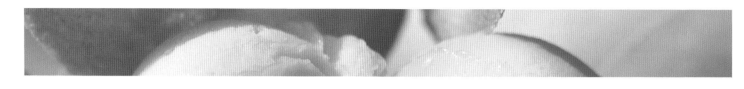

APRICOT SORBET WITH LAVENDER TUILES

A refreshing sorbet made with pungent fresh apricots. The biscuits are moulded in the shape of Provençal roof tiles (tuiles), hence the name.

Serves 6

SORBET

700 G/1½ LB RIPE APRICOTS, PITTED

JUICE OF 1 LEMON

15 ML/1 TBSP APRICOT BRANDY (OPTIONAL)

225 G/8 OZ/2 CUPS ICING SUGAR (CONFECTIONERS' SUGAR)

TUILES

50 G/2 OZ/¼ CUP BUTTER

2 EGG WHITES

125 G/4 OZ LAVENDER SUGAR (SEE NOTE BELOW) OR CASTER SUGAR (SUPERFINE SUGAR)

50 G/2 OZ/½ CUP PLAIN WHITE FLOUR (ALL-PURPOSE FLOUR)

3 HEADS OF LAVENDER, FLOWERS ONLY, PLUS EXTRA TO DECORATE

Place all the ingredients for the sorbet in a blender and process until smooth. Cover and chill for 2–3 hours (this means it will freeze more quickly), then freeze in an ice-cream maker for the best results. Alternatively, pour into a shallow freezer tray and freeze until the sorbet is almost firm. Mash well with a fork and refreeze until solid.

To make the tuiles, melt the butter and cool slightly. Whisk the egg whites until stiff, then whisk in the sugar a little at a time until the mixture is stiff again. Fold in the melted butter, followed by the flour and lavender flowers. Place teaspoonfuls of the mixture well spaced apart on a non-stick baking sheet – about 2 at a time. Sprinkle with extra lavender flowers and bake in an oven preheated to 190°C/375°F/Gas Mark 5 for 5–6 minutes, until golden brown. Oil a rolling pin. Lift the tuiles off the baking sheet as soon as they come out of the oven and drape them over the rolling pin to shape them. Leave to harden while you bake the next batch. Store in an airtight container.

Before serving, place the sorbet in the fridge for 30 minutes to soften. Serve scoops of sorbet with the tuiles.

NOTE

To make lavender sugar put 3–4 fresh or dried sprigs of lavender in a jar and cover with caster sugar (superfine sugar). Keep for at least 2 weeks before using.

NOUGAT

This exquisite confection of honey and nuts is easy to make if you have patience and a sugar thermometer! It is essential to the Treize Desserts – little dishes of grapes, apples, pears, dried apricots and figs, squares of quince paste, hazelnuts, walnuts, raisins, tangerines and two kinds of nougat, arranged around a sweet fougasse (see page 50) and traditionally eaten in Provence at Christmas.

Makes about
900 g/2 lb

200 G/7 OZ/1¾ CUPS BLANCHED ALMONDS
125 G/4 OZ/1 CUP SKINNED HAZELNUTS
250 G/9 OZ/1 CUP + 2 TBSP CASTER SUGAR
(SUPERFINE SUGAR)

225 G/8 OZ/1 CUP HONEY
3 EGG WHITES

Lightly oil a 1.1-litre/2-pint/5-cup loaf tin (bread pan) and line the base with rice paper or wax paper. Spread the almonds and hazelnuts on a baking sheet and place in a low oven just to warm through.

Put the sugar in a small, heavy-based saucepan and add 100 ml/4 fl oz/½ cup water. Heat gently until the sugar has dissolved, then bring to the boil and boil until it reaches 143°C/290°F on a sugar thermometer (candy thermometer). At the same time, heat the honey in a larger pan until it reaches the same temperature. Using a hand-held electric beater, whisk the egg whites until stiff. Mix the two hot syrups together in the larger saucepan and pour on to the egg whites in a thin, steady steam, whisking all the time. Return this mixture to the larger pan and cook over a gentle heat for 2–3 minutes. Stir in the warmed nuts. Pour into the prepared tin (pan) and place another piece of rice paper or wax paper on top. Place another loaf tin (bread pan) on top of the nougat and weight down with a couple of food cans. Leave to cool at room temperature, then turn out and cut into chunks or strips. Wrap in aluminium foil and store at room temperature for up to 1 month.

TARTE AU CITRON ET AMANDES

A classic lemon tart, but with the addition of ground almonds and a crust of flaked almonds – another of the bounties of this fruitful area of France.

Serves 6

PASTRY

225 G/8 OZ/2 CUPS PLAIN WHITE FLOUR (ALL-PURPOSE FLOUR)

30 ML/2 TBSP ICING SUGAR (CONFECTIONERS' SUGAR)

125 G/4 OZ/½ CUP BUTTER

2 EGG YOLKS

FILLING

2 EGGS

125 G/4 OZ/½ CUP CASTER SUGAR (SUPERFINE SUGAR)

ZEST AND JUICE OF 2 LEMONS

125 G/4 OZ/½ CUP BUTTER, SOFTENED

50 G/2 OZ/½ CUP GROUND ALMONDS

A FEW DROPS OF ALMOND EXTRACT

100 G/4 OZ/1 CUP FLAKED ALMONDS (SLIVERED ALMONDS)

To make the pastry, sift the flour and sugar into a bowl and rub in the butter. Stir in the egg yolks and enough iced water to bind to a firm dough. Knead lightly until smooth, then wrap in cling film (plastic wrap) and chill for 30 minutes. Use to line a 23-cm/9-inch fluted flan tin (tart pan), then chill again for 30 minutes. Bake blind for 15–20 minutes in an oven preheated to 190°C/375°F/Gas Mark 5.

To make the filling, whisk the eggs and sugar together until pale, thick and mousselike. Whisk in the lemon zest and juice, then whisk in the softened butter. Fold in the ground almonds and almond extract. Pour into the pastry case and scatter the almonds thickly on top. Bake at 190°C/375°F/Gas Mark 5 for 30 minutes, until set and golden. Serve warm, with crème fraîche if liked.

THE PROVENÇAL LARDER

GARLIC PURÉE

This is a good preserve to make if you have acquired a garlic 'grappe', or plait. This method will preserve it for much longer than hanging it in your kitchen. Stir the purée into soups and stews or just spread it on grilled bread.

Makes about 150 ml/¼ pint/ ⅔ cup

12 LARGE WHOLE HEADS OF GARLIC
SALT

30 ML/2 TBSP PROVENÇAL OLIVE OIL, PLUS EXTRA
TO COVER

Wrap the garlic loosely in a double layer of aluminium foil and bake in an oven preheated to 200°C/400°F/Gas Mark 6 for 1 hour, until completely tender. Open the foil and leave until the garlic is cool enough to handle. Separate the cloves and squeeze the insides out into a bowl. Beat in a little salt and the olive oil. Pass the mixture through a sieve, if you like, for a smoother consistency. Spoon into a jar and cover with a layer of olive oil. Refrigerate until needed. It will keep for up to 6 weeks, and can also be frozen for up to 3 months.

DRIED ORANGE PEEL

A good way to save the peel taken from oranges and tangerines after eating the fruit inside. It keeps indefinitely and adds a deep, earthy orange flavour to soups and stews.

Makes about 125 g/4 oz

1.4 KG/3 LB ORANGES OR SIMILAR CITRUS FRUITS

Score each fruit in quarters through the skin but do not cut the flesh; peel off the skin. Lay the skin on baking sheets and place in an oven preheated to 110°C/225°F/Gas Mark ¼ until completely dry – about 2 hours. Leave to cool completely before storing in an airtight jar. If you have an Aga, you can dry the peel in the bottom oven.

OVERLEAF: HARISSA AND BOTTLED TOMATOES

BOTTLED TOMATOES

A good way to preserve fresh tomatoes for the winter or for a special sauce. The tomatoes must be even-sized and not too ripe. Most of all they should have a good colour and flavour.

EVEN-SIZED SMALL OR MEDIUM TOMATOES

FRESH HERBS (OPTIONAL)

SALT

CITRIC ACID OR LEMON JUICE

Wash and dry the tomatoes, removing the stalks if liked. Pack into clean preserving jars (canning jars) with sprigs of herbs, if using. Top up with a brine solution made with 15 g/½ oz/2½ tsp salt to 1.1 litres/2 pints/5 cups water, adding 1.25 ml/¼ tsp citric acid or 10 ml/½ tsp lemon juice to every 450 g/1 lb jar. This is essential for preserving the tomatoes properly.

Seal the jars and place on a baking sheet lined with newspaper. Process in an oven preheated to 150°C/300°F/Gas Mark 2 for 1 hour–1 hour 10 minutes for 450 g–2 kg/1–4½ lb or 1¼–1½ hours for 2.25–5 kg/5–10 lb. Take out of the oven and allow to cool completely before wiping and labelling. Store in a cool, dark, dry place for up to 6 months.

SUN-DRIED TOMATO PASTE

This is really worth making at home if you have good tomatoes, especially if you grow your own – the flavour is superb!

Makes about 750 ml/1¼ pints/ 3 cups

1 KG/2 ¼ LB RIPE RED TOMATOES (PLUM IF POSSIBLE)

SALT

ABOUT 150 ML/¼ PINT/⅔ CUP PROVENÇAL OLIVE OIL, PLUS EXTRA TO COVER

Wash the tomatoes, then halve them horizontally and squeeze out most of the seeds. Lightly salt the insides and place upside down on a wire rack to drain for 30 minutes. Do not rinse. Arrange the tomatoes on racks in the oven and bake at the lowest setting for 8 hours or overnight, until shrivelled and dry but still pliable. Soak in warm water for 10 minutes and then drain (this makes them easier to purée). Place the tomatoes in a blender and blend until as smooth as possible, then blend in the olive oil until smooth again – you may need to add more oil. Spoon into jars and cover with a layer of olive oil. The paste will keep for 1 month in the fridge or can be frozen for up to 3 months.

BASIL PRESERVED IN OLIVE OIL

This is a great way to save basil when you are lucky enough to have too much or just want to make summer last longer! It is very good served with fish or used in salad dressings or sandwiches. It can also be used to make pistou or pesto.

Makes about 150 ml/¼ pint/ ⅔ cup

50 G/2 OZ/1 PACKED CUP FRESH BASIL LEAVES (NO STALKS)

SALT

PROVENÇAL OLIVE OIL

Pound the basil to a purée with a little salt in a pestle and mortar or process in a food processor until finely chopped. Blend with enough olive oil to give a thick paste. Spoon it into a jar and cover with a layer of olive oil. This way, the basil will retain its colour and flavour. It will keep in the fridge for 1 month.

CHERRIES IN EAU DE VIE

These are delicious served with vanilla ice cream – any liqueur left can be drunk in small glasses. Make them when cherries are in season and enjoy them as a treat at Christmas.

Serves 4

450 G/1 LB FIRM UNDERRIPE CHERRIES

ABOUT 1 LITRE/1¾ PINTS/4 CUPS EAU DE VIE, COGNAC OR ARMAGNAC

1 CINNAMON STICK

2 CLOVES

350 G/12 OZ PERFECT SWEET CHERRIES

125 G/4 OZ/½ CUP SUGAR

Pit the underripe cherries, crack the stones (pits) and place the cherries and cracked stones (pits) in a preserving jar (canning jar). Cover with the alcohol and stir in the cinnamon and cloves. Cover and leave to macerate at room temperature for 2 weeks.

Strain off the juices and reserve, discarding the cherry flesh and stones (pits). Wash the sweet cherries, dry and place in a large preserving jar (canning jar), filling it right to the top. Pour in the sugar and enough of the juice to cover the cherries completely. Seal tightly and leave to macerate for 1 month, lightly shaking the jar every now and then. The cherries will keep for 6 months.

HARISSA

Really worth making if you love spicy food, this North African spice paste livens up all tomato sauces. It is traditionally served stirred into couscous and is used a lot in Provence, whose cooking bears a strong North African influence.

Makes about
175 ml/6 fl oz/
¾ cup

50 G/2 OZ DRIED RED CHILLIES
2 GARLIC CLOVES, PEELED
SALT
5 ML/1 TSP CARAWAY SEEDS
10 ML/2 TSP CUMIN SEEDS

10 ML/2 TSP CORIANDER SEEDS
5 ML/1 TSP DRIED MINT
45 ML/3 TBSP PROVENÇAL OLIVE OIL, PLUS EXTRA
  TO COVER

Soak the chillies in hot water for 20 minutes until soft, then split them open and remove the seeds. Pat the chillies dry and place in a blender with all the remaining ingredients except the oil. Blend until beginning to form a paste. Blend in the oil and spoon the mixture into a sterilised jar. Level the surface and cover with more oil. It can be stored in the fridge for up to 2 months if kept covered with a layer of oil.

QUATRE ÉPICES

A spice blend used in all sorts of meat dishes, including sausages, pâtés, boudin blanc and daubes.

Makes about
60 ml/4 tbsp

45 ML/3 TBSP BLACK PEPPERCORNS
10 ML/2 TSP FRESHLY GRATED NUTMEG

5 ML/1 TSP GROUND OR WHOLE CLOVES
5 ML/1 TSP GROUND GINGER

Place all the ingredients in a coffee grinder or herb mill and blend to a fine powder. Store in an airtight container in a dark place for up to 4 months.

INDEX